ANCIENT JAPAN

Franklin Watts, Inc.
New York/1975

━━A First Book━━

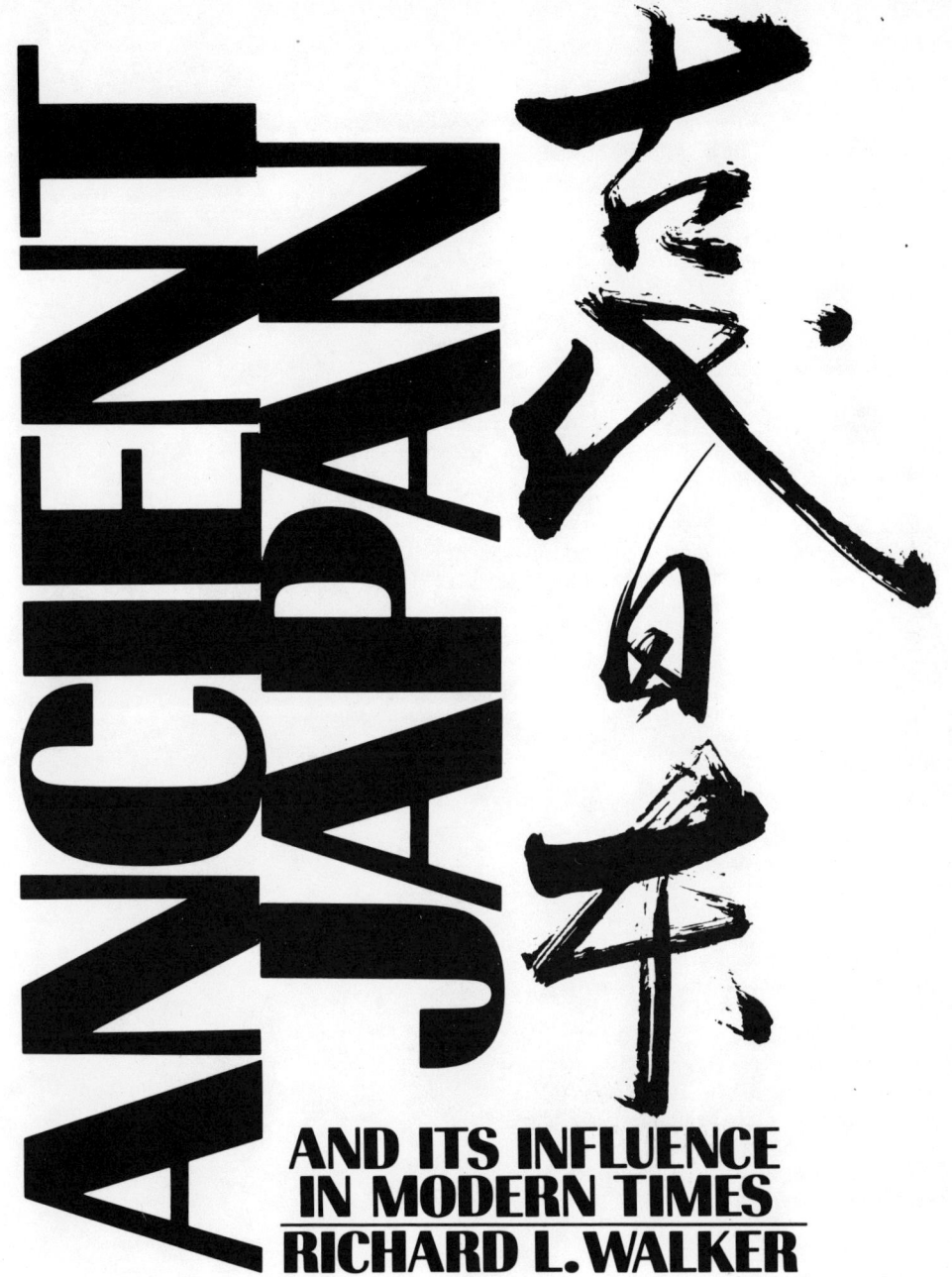

ANCIENT JAPAN

AND ITS INFLUENCE IN MODERN TIMES
RICHARD L. WALKER

Map by George Buctel
Cover design by One + One Studio
Cover line art by Minoru Morita

Pictures courtesy of: Consulate General of Japan, N.Y.: 3, 6, 9, 12, 15, 17, 25, 34, 40, 48, 57; *International Graphic* (Japan): 30; International Society for Educational Information, Tokyo, Inc.: 59; Japan National Tourist Organization: 22, 26, 54, 69, 72, 74, 76; The Metropolitan Museum of Art, John D. Rockefeller, III, Gift Fund, 1963: 64; Museo Oriental, Venice: 44; The New York Public Library, Picture Collection: 52–53; Tokugawa Art Museum, Japan: 39.

The *tanka* on page 41 is from *Anthology of Japanese Literature* by Donald Keene, copyright 1955, reprinted by permission of the publisher, Grove Press, New York.

Library of Congress Cataloging in Publication Data

Walker, Richard Louis, 1922–
    Ancient Japan and its influence in modern times.

    (A First book)
    Bibliography: p.
    Includes index.
    1. Japan—History—To 1600—Juvenile literature. I. Title.
DS850.W34   915.2′03′1   74-28238
ISBN 0-531-00827-4

Copyright © 1975 by Franklin Watts, Inc.
All rights reserved
Printed in the United States of America
5 4 3 2 1

CONTENTS

The Weight of
an Ancient Past:
Japan up to A.D. 538   1

Japan's Classical Age:
The Impact of China and
Buddhism up to 1184   20

The Militant Society:
The Achievement of the
Japanese Style up to 1600   46

Understanding
Traditional Japan:
Its Life and
Its Importance   66

Chronology of
Ancient Japan   79

Bibliography   81

Index   83

ANCIENT JAPAN

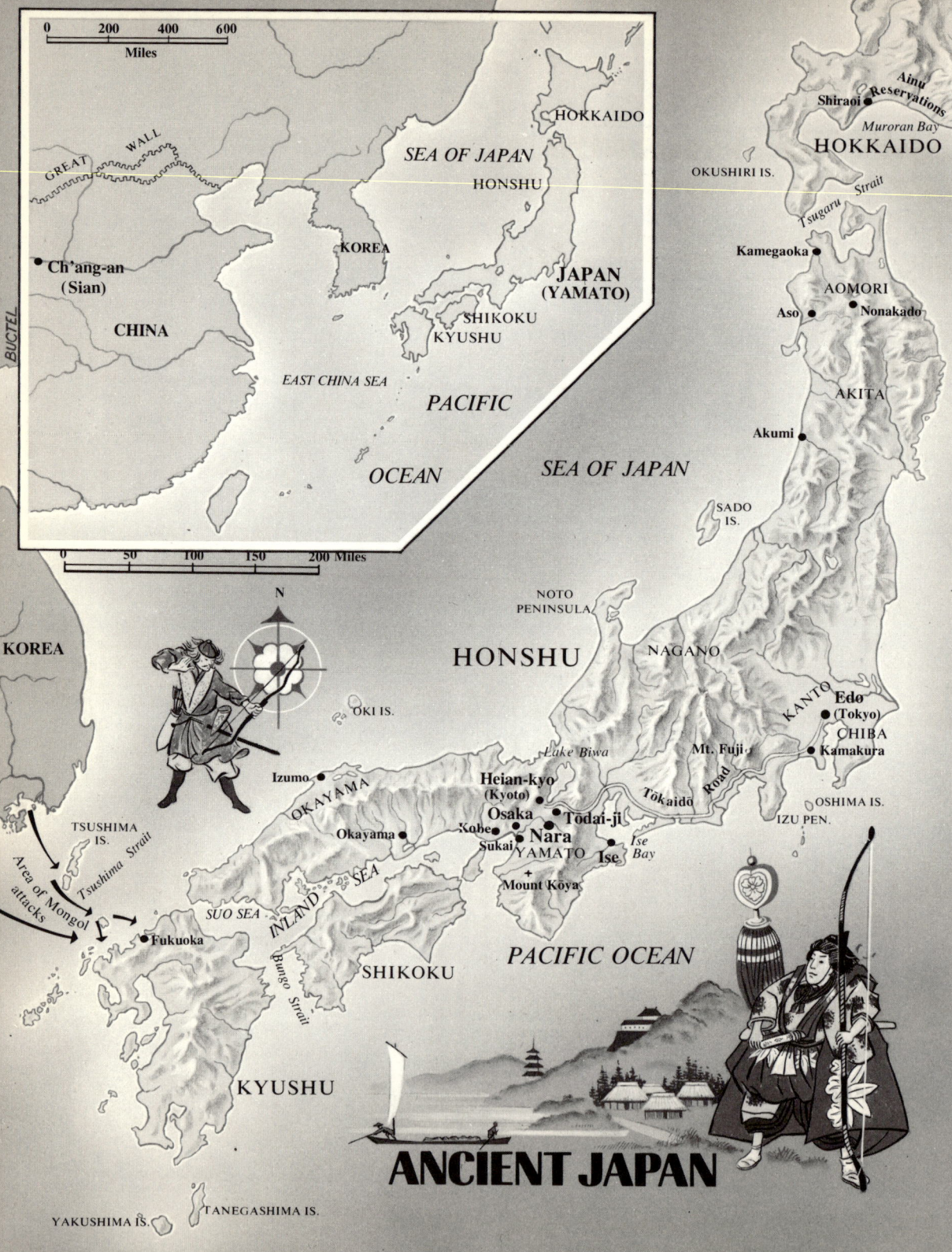

THE WEIGHT OF AN ANCIENT PAST
JAPAN UP TO A.D. 538

People who visit the island country of Japan today can only be amazed at this modern industrial and commercial miracle lying off the east coast of Asia. They can ride the famous Hikari Express, or "bullet train," from the old port town of Okayama to Tokyo at speeds of more than 125 miles per hour. Once in Tokyo, the world's most populous city, they will be impressed with the skyscrapers and rapid pace of life and marvel at the many ways in which the Japanese people utilize electricity, computers, transistors, and all the other developments of the scientific age. They could be justified in feeling that Japan seems to be the most thoroughly modern country in all of Asia or perhaps the world.

But this would only be partly true, for beneath the surface glitter of modernity are distinct patterns of Japanese life and culture that stem directly from the distant past. Probably no other modern nation bases so many aspects of daily life on traditions clearly rooted in its own ancient past. To understand the Japanese habits of cleanliness and discipline, to appreciate the Japanese approach to nature and its beauties, to learn about Japanese life and customs, it is necessary to look to the days of the distant past that set a mold that still persists. This mold can be discovered by anyone who is willing to observe the manner in which Japanese bow when they greet each other or to visit Japanese public gardens and shrines. Even in their busy lives Japanese workers or clerks are never far removed from the values of their country's past.

Today, when the modern Japanese businessman goes home at the end of the day, he quickly slips into a pattern of life that, except for some of the modern conveniences, would have been quite familiar to one of his ancestors of more than a thousand years ago. He leaves his shoes at the door rather than track dirt into his home, probably sheds his Western-style business suit for the more comfortable *kimono* (the traditional Japanese costume), and then settles down on a *tatami* mat in a cross-legged position. (Tatami are grass mats about three by six feet, which serve as standard flooring in the living areas of Japanese homes.) The family's food, the artistic manner in which it is served, and most of the decorations in the home have changed little over the centuries. The Japanese have always insisted on surroundings of subtle delicacy and good taste and, above all, simplicity.

The Japanese civilization is not very old when compared with those of Egypt or China, but the manner in which it has nourished and preserved the traditions from antiquity has made it older than most. The country's relative isolation from the rest of the world for long centuries led the people to concentrate on those values and patterns of conduct which they felt to be most vital in their frequent struggles with nature and geography. The Japanese learned from earliest times the importance of hard work and loyalty to a group or a larger task in their efforts to scratch a living from a frequently none too fertile soil. They also came to believe that they were a nation set apart and unique, and this gave them a feeling that they possessed a special destiny. An examination of Japan's past can quickly help us to see many dynamic factors that have made it the world's third greatest industrial and economic power, factors that lie rooted in an ancient past and continue, even in today's space age, to be consciously nurtured.

It is the Japanese *style* that has persisted over so many centuries—the art, the approach to nature and fellow humans, little actions, attitudes in society. All of these have retained much of the flavor of ancient times. What is more, the Japanese nation has managed to create a

Japanese home with tatami on the floor and sliding doors and walls

remarkable homogeneity among its people, and the unity has enabled them to feel that they share a national fate.

When the first Westerners—Portuguese Jesuit missionaries—encountered Japan in the middle of the sixteenth century, they were surprised by the country's remarkably high level of political and cultural development. They visited the capital city of the time, Kyoto, and marveled at its broad streets and beautiful temples and shrines. One of the missionaries estimated that there were more than 96,000 homes in a city of over half a million people, which made it grander than any city in Western Europe. The Jesuit fathers kept meticulous journals and sent back detailed reports about this country that captured their imagination and evoked their admiration.

The Jesuits noted, for example, the pride in the bearing of the men, the modest, soft-spoken manner of the women, the remarkable courtesy of the people, the tidiness and cleanliness on all sides, and particularly the discipline and attention to position in a society that set great store by rank and birth. Except for the breathtaking aspects of Japan's modernization, these are likely to be the same features a visitor to Japan would be inclined to comment on in the last quarter of the twentieth century.

The society the Jesuits came upon, like the Japan of today, was a fusion of forces from the unrecorded distant past and influences from the more easily available historical records of olden times—a fusion that is uniquely and distinctly Japanese. Some of the prehistoric forces, rooted in early habits of the people, must be understood because they have had such persistence in Japan. But first we must start with the people themselves.

We know from archaeological evidence that the Japanese people are a mixture of several strains—though the precise origins are far from clear. First, there was a group from the northern part of Asia who possibly moved to the Japanese islands while there was still a land bridge to the continent, tens of thousands of years ago. Because the

Japanese spoken language seems to be related to a central Asian family of languages, some linguistic experts feel that the Japanese people are related in prehistoric times to the tribes who once inhabited the area of the Ural Mountains, some of whom later moved westward into Finland and Hungary. Second, there were undoubtedly people of Mongoloid strains, possibly the ancestors of the Chinese, who found their way to the Japanese islands from Korea and the China coast. Third, there were the ancestors of the present-day Ainu people. These primitive Stone Age people are believed to have broken off from the white race at an early period and come into Japan by way of Siberia. They survived by hunting and fishing and were set apart from the Japanese through the centuries by the racial difference, evident in their greater body hair. Today the Ainu have been pushed into reservations on the northernmost island, Hokkaido, but they once occupied other areas of Japan. In fact, some specialists believe that it is the Ainu strain in the Japanese makeup that accounts for the Japanese having heavy beards and more hair on their bodies than the Koreans or the Chinese. There may also have been some strains from the areas of Southeast Asia mixed in with the Japanese inheritance. In any event, the melding of these races to make a homogenous Japanese people clearly took place before the Christian Era dawned.

One more touch was added, however, around the middle of the third century A.D. At about that time Japan was invaded by Mongol-type horsemen, probably related to the Huns who threatened the Roman Empire in distant Europe. Their fearsome abilities on horseback and their pride in their military arts probably enabled them to set themselves up as rulers over the natives. This in turn helped to provide Japanese society with a division between aristocrats and commoners, as well as an important respect for the warrior.

Whatever the racial mixture the Japanese nation is made up of, the early life developed in a somewhat tribal manner, with the various related groups who lived in the valleys along the Japanese coastline

Pottery figures of a dancing man and woman, called Haniwa, early masterpieces vividly depicting the joy of farmers

giving authority to chieftains and worshiping their own clan or tribal spirits. These clans or tribes, the *uji,* formed the basis for pride in family lineage, and it was the descendants of one of the most powerful *uji* in the Yamato area in southern Japan who were destined to become the imperial family of Japan—a house with one of the longest reigns in the world's history. In due course the *uji,* who initially inhabited self-contained small agricultural and fishing areas, began to specialize in other pursuits, such as military arts or religious functions, and to interact with each other. The powerful military *uji* eventually dominated the court of the reigning family in Yamato, but allowed it to continue as the symbol of the national unity. From the traditions of the *uji* come some of the most cherished patterns for the people: respect for a royal family that reigns but does not rule, loyalty to the group, and handing down of skills from generation to generation in families that keep meticulous genealogies.

Despite the divisions and rivalries created by the *uji,* the Japanese people had, by the early centuries of the Christian Era, become a distinct culture. Their mixed origins, however, may have accounted for some of the contradictions in their makeup. Some have felt that the Japanese have a split personality, and certainly aspects of this have been apparent in their later history. The Japanese can be sensitively appreciative of delicate beauty and can then in a flash exhibit a harsh and almost fierce bellicosity. They can be restrained and disciplined to the point of ignoring great pain in one moment and in the next burst into joyous laughter and be in good humor. They are capable at the same time of great concentration and attention to detail and flights of unrestrained fancy.

The Japanese have also fluctuated in their attitudes toward the outside world when they have encountered it, but they have always been open-minded and willing to learn. In fact, this characteristic of the Japanese people has been most frequently noted by foreigners, who often flatter themselves that the Japanese are copying them—and imitation is, after all, the highest form of flattery.

The Japanese attitude toward people and things from outside their country has frequently been described by the three words *adopt, adapt, adept.* The Japanese have shown a greater willingness than the people of most any other nation to adopt something that they see might be advantageous to them. But they then adapt it to their own society and geography rather than making a blind imitation. In due course they become adept at the skill or the practice involved, but by that time it is fully domesticated, fully Japanese. Even when in the most enthusiastic stages of adopting something from the outside—and probably they were enthusiastic about the martial arts of the invaders in the middle of the third century—the Japanese keep their own social organizations and customs intact. And after they adapt and become adept at something originally foreign, they are likely to close the door to further influences along that line. This pattern of approach—open adopting of foreign ideas and techniques and then closing itself off from the outside—by the Land of the Rising Sun (that is actually what the two syllables in the name *Japan* mean) has characterized the Japanese from earliest times. But whatever the Japanese did, they usually did it in unity as one people and as one nation.

Many of the characteristics of the Japanese must, of course, be associated with the special geographical situation of the country. This is the second important force in the Japanese tradition. Hokkaido, Honshu, Shikoku, and Kyushu: these are the four main volcanic islands, stretching from northeast to southwest, which constitute Japan, a country sufficiently far from mainland Asia to have permitted it to remain relatively isolated whenever it chose.

The islands are at once strikingly beautiful, ruggedly mountainous, and richly endowed with lovely little hidden valleys and a great variety of natural vegetation, including that most versatile of all plants, bamboo. Bamboo has been featured in Japanese art, architecture, and

Mount Fuji, highest mountain in Japan and a sacred symbol of the country through the centuries

practical household items from the very beginning of time. Near the great Kanto plain rises the spectacular 12,389-foot Mount Fuji, a perfectly shaped volcanic cone and a sacred symbol of Japan through the centuries.

With the exception of the northern island of Hokkaido, the climate of Japan is a moderate maritime one with four distinct seasons. But although Japan has adequate rainfall to supply the water needed for the cultivation of rice, the main crop, she has been less fortunate in other aspects of her geography. The islands lie directly in the path of those great Pacific hurricanes, the typhoons. (*Typhoon* is a Japanese word that means "great wind.") Typhoons lash the islands with great ferocity, causing great destruction by their powerful winds and through flooding. Too frequently the islands are shaken by great earthquakes, which also leave devastation and destruction. The Japanese soil is not exceptionally fertile, and less than one fifth of the limited land surface is suited for cultivation. Thus the Japanese have had to work in rugged and austere conditions. They have been disciplined by their surroundings, by the necessity for constant hard work for survival, and by the seasons. The four seasons have meant much in the Japanese tradition, and many festivals and celebrations are related to them. Japan is not a land richly endowed with natural resources, so it is not surprising that from earliest times values of thrift, austerity, frugality, and "making do" became part of the national character.

But if life was rough, there were other features that impressed themselves on the nation. The country is remarkably beautiful, full of woods, flowers, lakes, swift streams. The Inland Sea (lying between Honshu and Shikoku and Kyushu islands) is studded with green isles and attractive harbors. The people learned to approach their many scenic beauties with a sunny and happy nature and with a poetic spirit. Probably no people in the world have so consistently demonstrated, through their shrines, their gardens, and their approach to preserving natural beauties, their closeness to nature. Though nature could be at times harsh, the Japanese maintained an optimistic appreciation of the beauties it offered to mankind.

In fact, the third force from the prehistoric past that has carried through to the present is the manner in which the Japanese have put nature at the center of their lives. Early religion, customs, myths, and festivals were all built around the wonders of nature. The early *uji* developed an animist religion, which attributed divinity or a divine spirit, *kami,* to all things in nature, but especially to the lovely and the pleasant. Whether a rock, a tree, or flower, each had its own *kami*—pure and clean. Each *uji* had its own *kami* and felt especially close to the many *kami* or divinities in its own area of settlement. Religion was a happy thing in Japan, and the people frequently made special shrines of a beautiful spot on a mountaintop or an especially striking tree silhouetted against the sky.

Each shrine was identified, as it is still, by a gateway called a *torii*. The Japanese people would make food offerings at the little shrines they erected or identified. Because food was a scarce and valuable item, it came to symbolize the great depths of appreciation for a pleasant and beautiful work of nature.

Today tens of thousands of small shrines all over Japan call attention to this happy religious heritage from the past. Through the ages some standard patterns of worship developed, and some of the great shrines became more significant than others, but the basic features of Japanese *Shintō* have remained the same. *Shintō* means the "way of the gods or the *kami.*" The early Japanese believed that the *kami* were so pure that people should be clean in their presence. Thus the Japanese emphasis on cleanliness was closely related to the early religion. Purification by washing the hands and rinsing the mouth before clapping the hands three times in front of a shrine to attract the attention of the *kami* was the expected pattern. Because nature was as clean as a drop of dew on a fresh leaf in spring, the Japanese people knew that nature's gods expected cleanliness. Purification therefore became an im-

Torii, *or gates, mark Shinto shrines and are of very ancient origin. This torii, flanked by lanterns, is the gateway to Itsukushima Shrine*

portant part of the Shintō ritual. Emphasis on cleanliness also carried over into the home life of the people, who from earliest times stressed the importance of bathing. The Jesuits who came to Japan in the sixteenth century were astonished at the importance the people attached to bathing, which frequently took place in large communal baths.

The cult of cleanliness also led the Japanese to regard death as a sign of impurity. Thus in the pre-Christian era they had no permanent capital because, to escape from the impurity, it was deemed desirable to move the seat of government following the death of a ruler.

Within the framework of the many *kami* of Japanese animism, it is not surprising that a legend of creation is linked to them. Their myth about the origins of the Japanese nation and the ruling family has been elaborated by later stories, but much of it is probably based on historical fact and is related to the early movements and settlements of the people and the eventual creation of a center of authority and government in the Yamato area, near present-day Osaka, the industrial center of Japan. According to the myth, the country was founded by the grandson of Amaterasu, the sun goddess, who came down to earth with the three sacred symbols of authority: a mirror, a sword, and a curved jewel. These have subsequently become the symbols of the authority attached to the imperial family of Japan. Her great-great-grandson, Jimmu Tenno (*Jimmu* means "divine warrior"), again according to legendary account, became the first ruler of the Land of the Rising Sun in 660 B.C.

The linking of the government and the imperial line with the native cult of the *kami* enabled the Japanese to move more rapidly toward a national unity and sense of national consciousness, and this was hastened by the regular attention to the Shintō rituals. At Ise, a small peninsula in the Yamato area, and a beautiful site, is the most sacred spot for the followers of the "way of the gods," for it is here that the sacred mirror was reputedly moved in A.D. 5 and where the emperor and other high officials go to worship the sun goddess who founded their nation at her own shrine.

The Grand Shrine at Ise also demonstrates how the Japanese people cling to tradition. The simple wooden structures are moved and built anew approximately every twenty years, but they are meticulously copied after the original plan, which is a fairly early and primitive style. The buildings represent a style described in early Chinese accounts of Japan and pictured on bronze mirrors that have been excavated in recent years. In 1973 the Grand Shrine at Ise was reconstructed for the sixtieth time in more than thirteen centuries. Many of the workmen who followed the ancient plans, using ancient-style tools, could trace their ancestry through hundreds of years of craftsmen who had had the honor of building the shrine to Amaterasu. The peace and simplicity, and even the silence that seems to descend on noisy travelers when they arrive at Ise today, evoke an admiration for people who have managed to keep traditions alive for so long. The Grand Shrine at Ise, like the other great shrine at Izumo on the southwest coast of Honshu, is of great interest to those who study the customs of Japan and to those who are still trying to unearth more details of the earlier history.

In recent years archaeologists have been able to supplement the somewhat cloudy early legends with much more accurate information. They have developed a picture of Japan up to the fourth or fifth centuries of the Christian Era as a relatively primitive, isolated tribal country. By carbon-14 tests that measure radioactivity they have been able to date some of the early pottery remains scattered throughout Japan as approximately nine thousand years old. The culture of that time, known as Jōmon, which probably lasted for several thousand years, takes its name from the rope pattern, *jōmon,* on the pottery.

Ise Shrine. The building is rebuilt every twenty years exactly as it was originally designed; this is the fifty-ninth rebuilding

The few remains of the Jōmon period indicate that the people lived a rudimentary forest life with little in the way of fixed settlements.

The Jōmon culture was succeeded by the Yayoi period, which takes its name from the area not far from the center of present-day Tokyo where excavations first revealed the different type of society that replaced the Jōmon. *Yayoi* is an old Japanese word meaning the third month of the year, and this is probably a suitable description of the period, for it indicates a new springtime and youth for the Japanese. This period, which dates from about the third century B.C., witnessed the introduction of rice cultivation in the Chinese style and techniques of bronze and iron manufacture. Though Japan retained its relative isolation, there were obvious exchanges with the nearby continent, including importation of craftsmen and frequent visits by traders, probably from Korea. There were advances in building design too. Illustrations on some of the Yayoi bronzes show thatched roofs identical with some that can be seen in the Japanese countryside today.

By the middle of the third century A.D., more changes came, possibly sparked by the impact of the mounted horsemen of Mongoloid stock. Like the people of Korea and elsewhere in northeast Asia, the Japanese embarked on the construction of elaborate tombs for their chieftains. The period up to the middle of the seventh century is sometimes referred to by Japanese historians as the "tomb culture," after the many large tomb mounds dating from it. From the artifacts buried with the aristocratic leaders, a picture of a much more organized life for the Japanese people can be pieced together. During this time the village communities were solidly established, farmlands were regulated, and the society was more clearly divided into rulers and those ruled. Some of the aristocrats, judging from the tombs and the household and other items buried with the dead, lived rather luxurious lives. They were able to command the services of hundreds of Japanese commoners; they traveled on splendidly equipped horses

*An ancient model of an aristocrat,
excavated from a tomb*

and were well protected with expensive armor; and their houses were much finer than simple peasant huts.

The tombs in Japan reflect obvious influences from the Asian mainland. Yet there are indications that Japanese individuality was already asserting itself compared with the consistent pattern of tomb construction in nearby Korea; inside the tombs were pieces of pottery that are clearly related to the indigenous Yayoi culture. By their very size —some of the mounds are more than 1,500 feet long and 120 feet high—the tombs, many of which belong to the members of the imperial house, reflect a decided advance in the ability of political leaders to organize and carry through constructive enterprises.

There is yet one more force from the ancient past that helped to shape the unique character of the Japanese nation—Korea. As the great tombs in the southeast part of Korea make clear, there was a close and vital and almost continuous link between the Koreans and the nearby Japanese. Korea has always been a bridge to Japan across which flowed ideas and techniques from China and northern Asia. Though a national rivalry and pride have led the Japanese generally to deny or disregard Korea's role, recent archaeological work indicates that during the period of the "tomb culture" the Japanese were borrowing quite heavily from the Koreans. The Japanese in turn established colonies on the nearby Korean coast and may have passed along to the Koreans some of their own developments in tomb decorations.

The Koreans were, to be sure, indirectly under the influence of the great Chinese empire and had already learned the Chinese system of writing and other aspects of the high civilization of that great land. Koreans had been traveling to and from China for centuries and had moved to a position of being able to serve as the initial teachers for the Japanese in things Chinese: writing, painting, metal work, government, transportation, central taxation, census-taking. Though different from Japanese, the pattern of grammar of the Korean language made it easier than Chinese for the Japanese to learn. So Korea became, during the fifth and sixth centuries, a place that offered the Japanese an early introduction to the great cultural achievements of China. Many Koreans in turn migrated to Japan, where their skills enabled them to enter the ranks of the Japanese aristocracy. Starting from this period, the Japanese leaders were always sensitive about and interested in developments in Korea and showed special concern about keeping the Korean bridge open to traffic in both directions.

But Japan was to be profoundly affected by changes taking place in China during the sixth and seventh centuries. That great country had fallen into disunity and turmoil but was finally reunited by the dynamic Sui Dynasty, which brought it under rigorous control in A.D. 589. But the Sui measures proved to be too stern, and the dynasty was replaced by the T'ang, whose rule lasted almost three centuries, from A.D. 618 to 906. The T'ang provided a vigorous and golden age for China, when it led the world in many aspects of highly developed political, economic, and cultural life. There was much to be learned from China, and by the time the wonders of the T'ang Empire in China became known in Japan, the Japanese were at a point in their own development when they were ready to adopt, adapt, and become adept at what China had to offer.

JAPAN'S CLASSICAL AGE
THE IMPACT OF CHINA AND BUDDHISM UP TO 1184

From the early years of the Christian Era the Japanese had frequent, though irregular, direct contacts with the great Chinese empire. Chinese histories carry accounts of missions from the islands of the Rising Sun country to its court, as well as the observations of Chinese travelers in Japan. There had been basic knowledge of the high achievements of Chinese culture in Japan through direct trade and the exchange of missions. Japanese traders whetted the appetites of their people when they returned with Chinese coins and medicines, silks, mirrors, pottery, lacquer boxes, and household decorations. Such trade laid the foundation for what could be called the "Chinese fashion," which held Japan in full thrall beginning in the seventh century.

This "Classical Age" in Japan had its origins when in about A.D. 538 (the traditional date in most books is 552, which is probably inaccurate) a Korean king of one of the three kingdoms into which that country was then divided made a present of a gilt-bronze image of the Buddha and some Buddhist books to the Japanese court. The Korean king urged in a letter that Japan adopt Buddhism as the true faith for the salvation of the Japanese people. It was fitting that the Land of Morning Calm, Korea, should have taken the first important step toward the formal introduction of Buddhism and Chinese culture to Japan, because Korea had been the source of many developments in Japan up to that time and was to continue to be the most direct bridge for transmission of continental culture to the Japanese islands.

With the formal introduction of Buddhism and the language and culture of China, where the faith was most highly developed at that time, came the two most profound influences from the outside upon Japan until the impact of the West in the nineteenth century. These two influences may be likened to the two wheels of a cart. They speeded up the movement of Japanese culture and lent it direction, but though they were very important for the advances they made possible, the body of the cart was of Japanese construction, the road traveled was a Japanese road on Japanese land, and the guidance and direction were determined by the Japanese pulling the cart.

In the decades following the gifts and letter from Korea, numerous Buddhist monks came to Japan from Korea, and Japanese went across the narrow Tsushima Strait to Korea to learn the mysteries of this new religious inspiration from the Korean masters. By that time —the sixth century—the sun-goddess mythology and the development of Shintō as a state faith had already come about. It was to be expected that contests between the new religious impulse and the older religion would be intense. But here too the Japanese were to show their abilities at eclecticism—choosing and blending from various sources—and eventually the two faiths dovetailed neatly. Today in Japan the foreign observer might be puzzled that there are so many Shintō shrines and Buddhist temples side by side and that many of the gods in both seem to be the same, but this is perfectly understandable to the Japanese.

The important decision to adopt the Chinese model and the Buddhist faith that was so much a part of the Chinese scene then was made by a royal prince, Shōtoku, who acted as regent from 593 to 622, during most of the long reign of his aunt the empress. Shōtoku was an able leader, a highly educated man (meaning he was well schooled in the Chinese language and background), and a convinced Buddhist. Around the turn of the century he determined that Japan should adopt Buddhism as a state faith, that it should pattern its court and its conduct on the Chinese model, and that it should learn as much as

The Great Shintō Shrine at Izumo

possible from the Chinese. In 604 he issued what has become known as the "Seventeen Article Constitution" for Japan. Actually, the document was hardly a constitution as we understand the word, but rather a series of principles that he hoped the Japanese would accept. The first of these seventeen principles was a clear statement of the philosophy of the great Chinese teacher Confucius (551–479 B.C.), on which much of Chinese statecraft was based. It stated: "Harmony is to be valued, for when there is harmony between the ruler and the ruled and between neighbor and neighbor, what can not be accomplished?" The second of the seventeen principles urged acceptance of the "three sacred treasures" of Buddhism: the belief in Buddha, the acceptance of Buddhist law, and the commitment to service. Only one other of the seventeen articles need concern us here—most of the rest were like the Ten Commandments, principles for good conduct—and that is article twelve, which attempted to spell out clearly the authority of the royal family. It said the "sovereign is the master of the whole country, the officials to whom he gives control are his vassals."

Shōtoku approached his mission with a real vigor. He adopted the Chinese system of weights and measures; he initiated the utilization of the Chinese calendar, which is still used in Japan today for ceremonial purposes; and he attempted to establish Chinese-style court ranks. Prince Shōtoku was totally enthusiastic about having his country learn the high civilization of the Middle Kingdom (the name that the Chinese people gave their country).

Shōtoku attempted to make Buddhism a state faith. He did not try to force his people to make it the one and only faith, but he acted under the Chinese philosophy that the rulers should set the example for the people and they would naturally follow. But if his goal was to bring his people to accept the great religious faith of Buddhism, he realized that this would mean learning the highly difficult Chinese language and borrowing much from China. However, there was no reason to be concerned about this, because after all, the Chinese people themselves, who had one of the highest of cultures, had not hesitated to accept a foreign religion and adapt it to their environment. (Buddhism had come originally from India.) The prince entered into his task of exposing his people to Chinese culture and to Buddhism with unbounded enthusiasm. He lent impetus to the building of temples and the importation of teachers and techniques for their adornment. In 607 he began the construction of the Hōryū-ji, one of the most famous temples in all Japan. Its Golden Hall, which still survives from Shōtoku's time, is reputed to be the oldest wooden building in the world; certainly it is one of the most graceful, and the warmth of the old wood gives a modern-day visitor a feeling of closeness to the traditions of early Japan. Many of the images, which were carved and cast at Shōtoku's behest, remain in the Hōryū-ji, and have been declared national treasures of Japan.

It may seem strange on the surface that the Japanese should have taken so enthusiastically to a religion that had its origins in India and that contained so much obscure philosophical speculation alien to the wordly Japanese national character. But there were features of the faith that were well suited to the natural conditions in Japan. The Buddha, who was an Indian contemporary of Confucius, had accepted the Hindu belief in reincarnation. This belief held that the soul was permanent and was born again and again in different forms—animal, insect, or human—depending upon moral conduct in this world. Buddha taught, however, that there was a path to release from such a fate, and that path was through the elimination of desire, through service to mankind, and through such principles as returning good for evil. The goal was an eventual condition of peace, called *nirvana,* where the soul would be without desire and would be liberated from the fate of endless rebirths.

The Chinese had changed many of the more mystical qualities of Buddhism as they embraced it during the first centuries of the Christian Era. Most important, they had begun to worship the Bodhisattvas,

*The Hōryū-ji temple, built in Chinese style,
is the oldest wooden building in the world
and certainly one of the most graceful*

or those who attained the "enlightened existence" and paused at the threshold of *nirvana* long enough to assist weaker creatures to attain salvation. One of the Bodhisattvas, Amida, became the great savior ready to assist all who worshiped to attain entrance into his "Western Paradise," or "Pure Land." A Bodhisattva attendant of Amida, known to the Japanese as Kannon, was gradually transformed by the Chinese and Japanese into the female "Goddess of Mercy" who was always full of compassion and help for mortals who turned to her. Various sects developed in China and Japan, each with its own approach to winning the help of Amida Buddha (in Japanese, *Amida Butsu*) for salvation. One Japanese sect taught that it was only necessary to repeat the name of Amida a sufficient number of times. His grace was presumably bountiful enough to bring salvation from the trials and miseries of earthly life. Genshin (942–1017), one of the later teachers who extolled the importance of Amida, did much to popularize Buddhism among the lower classes in Japan.

Despite its Indian mysticism, several aspects of Buddhism did appeal to the Japanese national character. They were emphasized in various ways by the diverse sects that existed, and still exist, side by side almost from the beginning. In the first place, the Buddhist teaching that salvation could be attained by restraint, discipline, and an austere and simple life fitted the Japanese traditional value pattern. Hope for miracles and answers to prayers in the harsh conditions of early Japan lent attraction to the Buddhist ritual. The beautiful temples, images, and art works associated with the faith provided an outlet for native artistic abilities. The elaborate ceremonies with prayers and incantations verging on magical promises of rewards made some of the sects particularly welcome in Japan. The variety in ap-

An early and delicate statue of a Bodhisattva,
a Buddhist deity who waits to help those
along the path to nirvana, *the Buddhist heaven*

proaches to Buddhist truth enabled the Japanese to fit some of their own Shintō *kami* into the scheme of this new religion. Buddhism was in essence a force that could be melded into the Japanese scene and, therefore, they adopted it with enthusiasm.

Japan became from the eighth century onward a thoroughly Buddhist country and remained so until modern times, more so than either China or Korea, from whom it had learned. Buddhism in turn had a profound impact on Japan. It was for more than a thousand years the chief inspirer of Japanese art, architecture, aspects of literature, and even the subtleties of Japanese gardening. Some of the greatest political leaders through the centuries were Buddhist clerics. A good example of how Buddhist doctrine fitted in with Japanese predispositions and in turn influenced Japanese customs lies in the fact that, from the middle of the seventh century on, the Japanese abandoned their ancient burial rites and switched to cremation of the dead—a Hindu tradition. This was not only harmonious with the Buddhist view that the soul passes into another form but more congenial to the Japanese custom that had tended to regard the dead as impure—fire cleansed the impurities away.

The Japanese forms of the "religion of infinite compassion," as Buddhism has sometimes been described, tended to become more and more national in character with the passing of time, but the leaders in the Land of the Rising Sun were anxious to get the full benefit of the knowledge from China before they began the final process of digesting it. Beginning with a first expedition launched by Shōtoku in 607, they sent many great missions to China to learn everything possible about the new religion, and, in addition, to trade and bring back other Chinese products. These missions, across treacherous seas, sometimes ended in shipwreck and disaster, for in the seventh and eighth centuries the techniques of navigation and shipbuilding were not as highly developed as the thirst for Buddhist knowledge. But most were successful in bringing back ideas and inspiration from

China. Many of the key Japanese leaders of the faith spent years in China studying and absorbing aspects of Buddhism and its arts. The last of the great missions to China was sent in 838. After that, disorder in the Middle Kingdom made the expeditions dangerous and, besides, the Japanese had by that time enough to assimilate. Two of the most important Buddhist sects in Japan today were founded by student monks who accompanied an official mission sent by the Japanese to China in 804; these monks were Kūkai, who founded the Shingon ("True Word") sect and established a monastery on Mount Kōya on the south of the Yamato plain in 816, and Saichō, who introduced the Tendai sect and founded a rival monastery on a mountain north of the plain. These two monasteries became important religious centers in Japan. With the teaching of the monks and the acquisition of major headquarters, the Japanese Buddhists were in a position to make further adjustments of their faith to the local scene. Part of this involved entering into the stream of political and economic development of Japan. Many of the sects and their estates became powerful and wealthy, because they were granted the privilege of tax-free status, and later some of them were to become important enough to field their own armies for the protection of their temples and their holdings. Buddhism, therefore, became so enmeshed in Japanese society and history following the time of Shōtoku that it is impossible to understand Japan or the Japanese people without some knowledge of this religion, which has influenced more people than any other in the world. Buddhist patterns and faith lie beneath the modern surface glitter of Japan today and deeply influence politics and society.

Equally significant in the development of Japanese culture and society was the influence of China itself. The political and cultural institutions of the Middle Kingdom held great attraction for the Japanese, and the enthusiasm for borrowing from China and for things Chinese seemed fully to match the Buddhist ardor, especially at the

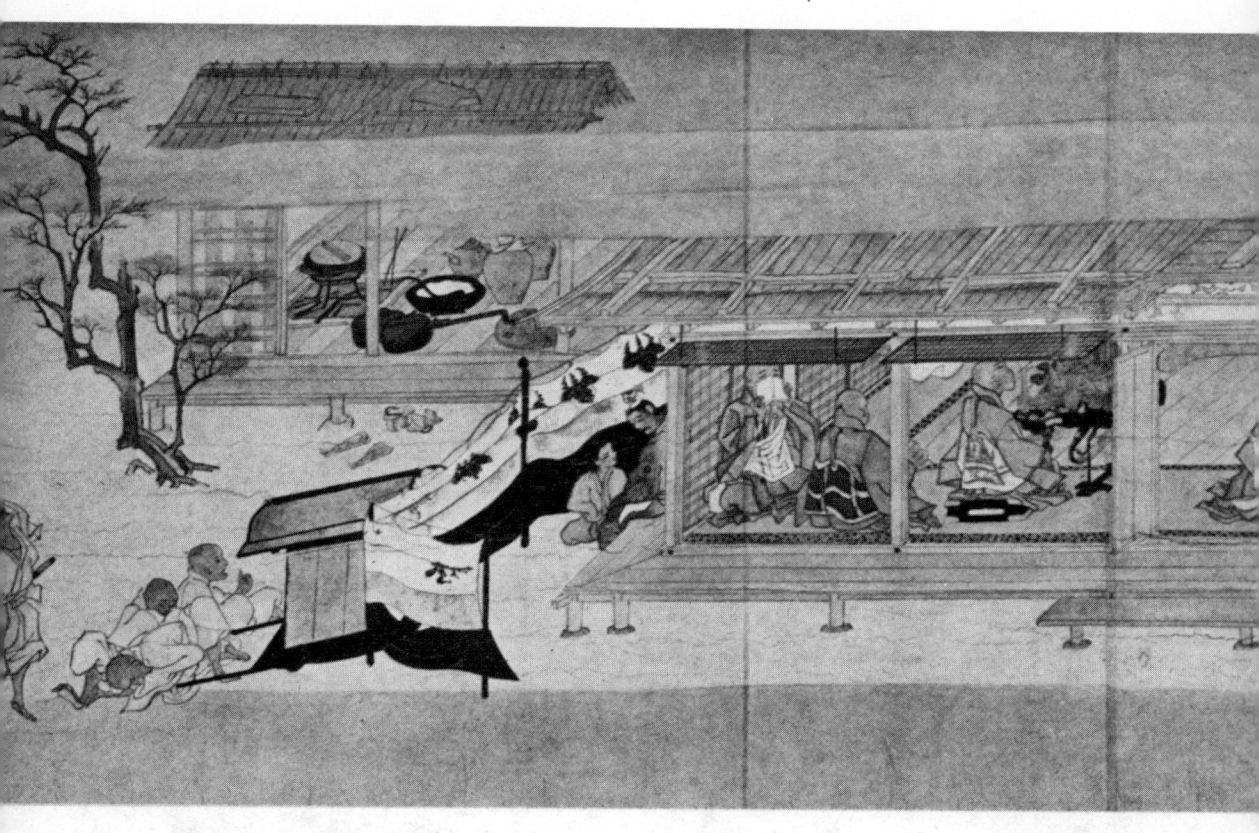

「法然上人繪傳」 東京・芝増上寺藏 （二卷傳その一）

Life in a monastery

Japanese court. In order to understand this, it is necessary to know about the China of the T'ang Dynasty (618–906) and its capital.

With the dawning of the T'ang era, China entered into one of its most productive and vital ages. The great empire was ruled by a well-selected bureaucracy based on a civil service examination system and the learning of Confucian classics and ideals. Its capital Ch'ang-an, the present-day city of Sian, was one of the greatest cosmopolitan centers the world had seen up to that time. To it came monks from India, rulers from Persia, traders from Arab lands, and diplomats from the Byzantine Empire. The city itself was mammoth in scale, more than thirty square miles, and may have had close to two million people. In its marketplace were spoken all the languages of central Asia. Leaders of most of the major religions of the world—Nestorian Christians, Moslems, Hindus, and Buddhists—met there. Of all the religions Buddhism was the most fascinating for the Chinese, not only because of its teachings but because it offered them clues to the languages of India and central Asia.

Ch'ang-an, one of the most colorful of Oriental courts, was the center for lavish spectacles. The T'ang court was the scene of poetry contests and the home of some of the greatest painters China produced. Its influence, intellectual and artistic activity, and political power were felt from Japan to the shores of the Caspian Sea. So great was the esteem for learning and scholarship among the Confucian scholar-rulers that a gentleman's library might have as many as ten thousand printed volumes. (This was at the time of the so-called Dark Ages in Europe, when a major library there might have only as many as fifty parchment scrolls or volumes, all hand-inscribed.) The beauties of the poetry of T'ang Dynasty China were to prove especially attractive to those Japanese who eventually learned the complex Chinese language, and they had much literature to choose from. One of the Chinese collections of poems of the T'ang Dynasty (now available in most large libraries in the world) contains almost fifty thousand well-known poems by some twenty-two hundred poets of the period. Equally impressive in Ch'ang-an were its palaces, parks, and pavilions. Little wonder, then, that the Japanese turned to T'ang China and made its capital their model.

The enthusiastic full-scale borrowing from China on the foundation laid by Shōtoku began with the Taika, or Great Reform, of 645–650, under a royal prince and his chief minister, Nakatomi no Kamatari. Kamatari's zest for China was matched by his brilliance, and he left an impact on Japan that makes him one of the great men in Japanese history. In fact, the prince who was later to become the Emperor Tenchi rewarded his powerful minister by bestowing upon him the new family name of Fujiwara; the name was taken from the Fujiwara district, where the prince also gave him land. The bestowing of a new family name was considered a great honor. The Fujiwara family was to dominate the court for the next three and a half centuries. The imperial family reigned, but the Fujiwara and their successors actually ruled. This tradition of indirect rule, as much as any, may have helped to protect and perpetuate the royal family in Japan, since there were seldom power contests or battles for a position that had little real say in the affairs of state.

The Taika of Kamatari also brought the provinces under nominal control of the central government, on the pattern of the Chinese empire. This was always a goal of the rulers behind the throne, and by the ninth century the official registers listed sixty-six provinces grouped in turn into circuits or *dō,* also in Chinese fashion. One of the most famous of these was the Eastern Seas Circuit or Road, the Tōkaidō, which was the major road linking the provinces from the Kanto plain, where Tokyo is situated today, to the Yamato region. It is this ancient *dō* that the modern "bullet train" follows from Tokyo to Kyoto. The Taika also attempted to nationalize land and systematize taxation. In effect, what Kamatari did, in his imposition of Chinese organization, was to replace many of the tribal and local patterns with official and central ones. He was, of course, only partially successful. Many of the provinces continued to maintain their independence, giving only nods in the direction of the royal court and interested in it only for the entertainment and splendor that it offered them during their visits. The Chinese concept of a civil service based on merit rather than birth also failed to take hold in a land where family lineage and royal descent meant so much. Nevertheless, Kamatari's efforts did start the Japanese state on the path toward a national government.

His efforts were followed by the establishment of Japan's first official capital, Nara, in 710. Not surprisingly, the city was laid out in a pattern somewhat smaller than, but almost identical to, Ch'ang-an, and the new Japanese capital soon acquired all the trappings of its Chinese model. Pilgrims and students who had just returned from China were given high positions. Artists were imported and scholarship was encouraged. Under the direction of the court, official histories of the country were compiled. Two of these, the *Kojiki,* or "Ancient Records," completed in 712, and the *Nihongi,* or "Japanese Chronicle," of 720, combined the mythology about Amaterasu, the sun goddess, and her descendants, dating back to 660 B.C., with accurate traditional data, and so they have become some of the first printed source books on Japanese history. It is suspected, however, that the Japanese compilers were trying to match the splendor and antiquity of the Chinese, whose history they had learned.

The Nara period began a burst of artistic and building activity on the Chinese model that was to last more than a century and a half. The artists in Nara cast a vast bronze Buddha some fifty-three feet high. It and the Great Buddha, *Daibutsu,* at Kamakura remain the two greatest bronze statues in the world. The Nara Buddha is housed today in the impressive Great Hall of the Tōdai-ji, or Great Eastern Temple, the largest wooden building in the world, and was dedicated with great fanfare in 752. The power of the Buddhists was illustrated by their ability to gather the copper, lead, gold, tin, and energies for

such a large construction. The gilding of the statue is said to have taken more than five hundred pounds of gold. Small wonder, therefore, that three quarters of a century after the founding of Nara, the Emperor Kammu decided to move the capital away from the influences of the Buddhist priests and sects. After an unsuccessful attempt at an interim location, he settled on an area in the Yamato plain, which he called Heian-kyo, or the "Capital of Peace and Tranquillity." Heian, founded in 794, was destined to remain the seat of the imperial Japanese family and the nominal capital of the land until 1868, more than a millennium. There building and artistry continued to reflect the enthusiasm for T'ang China.

Kammu's new capital was laid out on an even grander scale than Nara—it was a rectangle about three miles by three and one-half miles —and was an even closer approximation to the Chinese capital at Ch'ang-an. Heian, later known simply as "the capital," or by its present name, Kyoto, became the center of court life and national development while the Japanese were adapting things Chinese and Buddhist to their own environment. Initially there was an almost single-minded determination to mimic the Chinese. The Heian court copied costumes, rank, poetry, painting, and even music. Today Japan, rather than China, retains the court music and dances of T'ang China. Each new expedition, bringing back more Chinese creations and models, was a major event in the life of the capital. For almost three hundred years an artificial court life of great sophistication in ceremony and costume centered around the palace on which more than 300,000 laborers had worked at one time.

Life in Heian-kyo, for three centuries following its founding, was elegant and cultured for the few thousand members of the aristocracy, and most of the activities of the remaining hundred thousand inhabi-

*The Great Buddha of
the Tōdai-ji at Nara*

tants of the city were devoted to serving them, pampering them, and making them comfortable. The paintings and accounts that have survived show us elegance and refinements clearly inspired by the Chinese. In fact, the traditional Japanese costume, the long and flowing kimono, stems from the fashions of the T'ang court.

So faithful were the Japanese in their copying of Chinese art and architecture that Nara and Kyoto are regarded today as the major centers of preservation of creations in the T'ang dynasty style. While most of the old T'ang wooden temples and many of the greatest Chinese art treasures have been lost or destroyed, in Japan they or their copies have been preserved. It is in these first two Japanese capitals and their monuments, so conscientiously preserved by tradition-bound Japanese, that we can taste the flavor of Chinese life about which the poets wrote. The Chinese and their island neighbors who learned from them developed to a high peak of beauty the construction of wooden buildings, maintaining grace and openness combined with attractive decoration and a form that blended with natural surroundings. People from all over the world journey to Kyoto and Nara today to admire the buildings and art treasures dating from Japan's Classical Age.

Perhaps the most challenging task for the Japanese was to adapt the Chinese written language to the Japanese speech. The Chinese had developed a symbolic written script, which required an enormous investment of time and energy to learn. Chinese has no alphabet, and the literate person must memorize thousands of graphs, or "characters." The Chinese characters are geared to a language that emphasizes tonal differences in speaking and in turn reflect the thousands of years behind their development. Japanese, on the other hand, is a language with a few simple sounds and a complex grammar. Fitting the written Chinese symbols to Japanese sounds and meanings seemed almost impossible. Initially the Japanese aristocrats treated writing as just another skill like carpentry or weaving and recruited scribes to write their notes or messages for them. But eventually, in a court that set such great store by China, the learning of the Chinese characters became essential. The earliest of the Japanese works dating from the Nara and Heian periods were thus composed in Chinese. The Japanese at the court even competed in writing Chinese poems in the Chinese style and using writing brush techniques in art work. Most of the paintings during the Nara and early Heian period were copies of styles then in vogue in China.

The use of Chinese tended to separate the court nobility from the mainstream of Japanese life, and in due course, as might be expected, some Japanese began to turn to their own language and its possibilities. Gradually certain standard Chinese characters came to represent Japanese sounds. These were in turn abbreviated in written style, and eventually from this practice there emerged in the ninth century two sets of symbols, the *katakana* and the *hiragana,* both known simply as *kana,* to stand for the forty-seven simple syllables of the Japanese language. Once the Japanese had made this step forward toward a semi-alphabet, or *syllabary,* they were ready to move from the Chinese written language and develop their own national literature and art. Their products remained intimately linked, however, to many Buddhist and Chinese values.

The development of the *kana* syllabary quickly had an impact on Japanese art and letters. Whereas the paintings and literature from the founding of Nara in 710 until the middle of the ninth century were in Chinese court style, from then on the Japanese spirit began to express itself. Calligraphy, the artistic writing with a disciplined brush, began to be expressed in flowing and less detailed lines. It has always remained an important art form in Japan.

Female diarists used the new Japanese script to write detailed accounts of the life of high society. In the Heian period, women played an important part in Japan's life and politics. (It was not until much later that they were reduced to an almost servile role.) Two of the great Japanese classics illustrate this fact as well as the literary trend. The first is the *Pillow Book* of Sei Shōnagon, a collection of witty and sometimes critical comments on the people and customs at the court by a talented woman, written about the year 1000. The other, written by Lady Murasaki around 1020, is truly one of the most famous works of literature in the whole world. It is called *The Tale of Genji*. This very long work is the world's first novel and deals with the affairs of a remarkable young man, Prince Genji, during one of Japan's fascinating times of turbulence. Lady Murasaki wrote with grace, poetic elegance, psychological insight, and a remarkable ability to capture the Japanese flavor. Her work has justly been acclaimed as Japan's greatest literary classic.

Not surprisingly, such works as *The Tale of Genji* in turn inspired new developments in Japanese painting and art. Once the Japanese artists broke away from mimicking the T'ang masters, the style became known as the Yamato style of painting, meaning Japanese, because Yamato had by then become another name for Japan. Native stories and novels were illustrated by *makimono,* or picture scrolls, some of the most famous of which naturally depict episodes from *The Tale of Genji,* and were painted in striking color in the twelfth century. From the mid-ninth century, Yamato art also featured quaint single-sheet pictures of everyday life and people, some drawn with quick brushstrokes, almost cartoons and caricatures. Japanese artists have retained to this day the ability to capture a significant or humorous mood or moment by a quick sketch.

Kana also made possible the development of native Japanese poetic art. Japanese poetry also expressed the national character so completely that translation becomes almost impossible. The poems are usually short, with a defined number of syllables, and within the restraints laid down, the poet attempts to capture a scene, a mood, a piquant moment, or a natural wonder in such a way as to stir emotional response and to stimulate the mind to capture an instant picture, complete with sound and color.

The earliest collection of more than four thousand Japanese poems

Scene from the picture scroll of The Tale of Genji

Picture-scroll painting of hares and frogs amusing themselves by mimicking a wrestling match, showing the Japanese sense of line and caricature

was made toward the end of the Nara period, before the development of *kana*. This work, the *Manyōshū*, or "Book of Ten Thousand Leaves," is one of the earliest literary classics. It is the product of court aristocrats trained in Chinese, and the complex Chinese characters are employed in irregular fashion to represent Japanese syllables. Little wonder the Japanese began to standardize and simplify their writing system. Nevertheless, many of the poems in the *Manyōshū* are strictly Japanese in flavor, particularly the *tanka* or "short poems." These poems of thirty-one syllables are divided into groups of 5, 7, 5, 7, and 7 syllables and offer a real challenge to the poet who wishes to catch a scene or a moment in impressionistic fashion. *Tanka* represented a type of intellectual game that appealed to the Japanese, and they became the most important poetic style for centuries.

The *tanka* in the *Kokinshū*, or "Collection of Ancient and Modern Poems," compiled by imperial direction in 905, were written for the most part in *kana* and represent the Japanese style of subtle suggestion and allusion at its best, within a defined restraint of thirty-one syllables. The poems in the *Kokinshū* also illustrate the developing Japanese approach to beauty. The aesthetic code in Japan came more and more to be that beauty must not be paraded but, as in nature, lie beneath the surface to be discovered in a moment of inspiration by one's true artistic spirit. This approach has lain behind the delicate subtlety of Japanese painting, gardens, architecture, literature, and other arts up to this very day. Perhaps one can gain a small idea of the flavor in the following *tanka* from the *Kokinshū,* together with its thirty-one Japanese syllables:

Hisakata no	This perfectly still
Hikari nodokeki	Spring day bathed in the soft light
Haru no hi ni	From the spread-out sky,
Shizu kokoro naku	Why do the cherry blossoms
Hana no chiruramu	So restlessly scatter down?

In the Heian period the Japanese also gradually developed their own political style. Those Chinese institutions that did not fit native traditions were discarded; others were modified. Much of the credit for the initial political adjustment belongs to the Fujiwara descendants of Kamatari. One of them, Yoshifusa, who became head of the family in 857 and was appointed grand minister of state, ensured that members of his family dominated and led the government in succeeding generations. From his time on, the Japanese turned away from China and in to themselves. During this period of modification and cultural flowering, the Fujiwara clan gave the inhabitants of Kyoto almost three centuries of effective civil rule. Many historians call the period from the founding of Heian in 794 until 857 the Heian period and distinguish it from the Fujiwara period, or Later Heian period, which lasted until 1155 when three decades of military struggle between two families, the Minamoto and the Taira, began over who was to rule in the name of the imperial family. By that time some major social and political changes had taken place.

While affairs in the fabulous capital city with its beautiful palaces and temples were being recorded in poetry and novels by pampered aristocrats, life in the provinces continued to be primitive and rugged. The peasants and fishermen lived in the crudest shelters with straw scattered on mud floors on which the family huddled together to keep warm during half the year. Of the five million people in the Japanese islands during the Heian period, few indeed had enough food to tide them over the winter months in comfort. The peasant families labored from sunrise to sunset with few pleasures and little entertainment. Often a man in the household would be called away to do forced labor in helping to build the residences for the aristocrats or to do battle on the frontier, and the rest of the family would have to do the absent man's share. If a peasant family managed to build a little reserve of grain or coarse cloth, there was always a tax collector to make demands.

The poor country people of Japan were heavily taxed by their landlords in order to pay for life at court or in the provincial towns, and frequent famines led to marauding bands invading from one province or estate to another. Gradually provincial barons took on more and more responsibility for protecting their lands and their peasantry, and the smaller landholders sought the protection of the greater ones by pledging allegiance to them, becoming in effect their knights. For the protection of the great *shōen,* tax-free estates or manors, there gradually emerged in the later Fujiwara period a warrior caste who were to have such an important part in Japanese social and political development.

Rivalry developed between the great regional *shōen* and clans, and some of them began to maintain their own personal armies of knights and conscripts. The most prominent families on the immense estates were later to become the *daimyō* ("great names") or powerful regional and provincial military lords in Japanese history. When the famous struggle between the Minamoto and the Taira families erupted in full force, the Fujiwara were already declining in vigor, and it was clear that military rivalries were more important than political rivalries at the court. Battles between the families dated far back; one of the first great ones lasted from 1028 to 1031. In the course of the campaigns, such as those that raged over the islands of Honshu and Kyushu, the peasants frequently suffered devastation and plundering. In the following century, provincial warriors of aristocratic descent, *bushi,* gradually gathered around the two great rival families. Battles raged through the early part of the twelfth century until 1160, when it seemed that the Taira chief, Kiyomori, had won the power to direct the national fortunes from behind the imperial throne.

Kiyomori did not, however, eliminate all of his rivals, and after he settled down in Kyoto, the Taira cause seemed to have lost some of its zest. He died in 1181. Four years later the great Minamoto leader Yoritomo, who had been building new headquarters in the Kanto area,

Detail of an eighteenth-century painted screen showing scenes from the Taira and Minamoto wars

succeeded in routing the Taira leaders from the capital and driving them to the southwestern tip of Honshu, where they were annihilated in a great sea and land battle. Yoritomo's victory in 1185 launched a new era in Japanese history.

The more than a century of fighting between the shifting alliances headed by the Taira and the Minamoto has been considered one of the great periods in Japanese history. Most young Japanese study the period with enthusiasm because of the romantic legends connected with it. The Chinese-style pronunciation of the characters of the Minamoto name is Genji, and thus this family, which was first given its name by the emperor Saga in 814, was the subject of Lady Murasaki's famous novel. Perhaps her intuition foresaw the remarkable period that Yoritomo's victory was to usher in.

THE MILITANT SOCIETY
THE ACHIEVEMENT OF THE JAPANESE STYLE UP TO 1600

Over the centuries following the establishment of Kyoto, there had developed a deepening contrast between life in the royal capital and that in the rest of the countryside. As the warriors around the manors of local leaders began to place more emphasis on discipline and training in the arts of fighting, some of them showed little respect for the effeminate leaders in Kyoto who, for example, in the eleventh century were spending time and effort in mixing just the right perfumes so that each prince might be recognized by his own specially blended scent. Thus the farther one got away from the capital, the stronger were likely to be reactions against its signs of weakness, both physical and moral. In the provinces near the Kanto plain and further to the northeast there were still battles to be fought against the fierce aboriginal Ainu. In the provinces of Kyushu a warrior tradition also had a firm foothold.

When Yoritomo won his decisive victory over the Taira in 1185, there was every expectation that the monks and warriors at the militant power centers would continue to challenge his authority on the field of battle and would try to enmesh him in the debilitating politics of the capital. But this brilliant commander, with a sense for the political institutions demanded by the times, decided to set up his headquarters far away from Kyoto, where the soft life of the court had helped to undermine his Taira rivals. He also determined to keep the country on a war footing or an alert status, so to speak, so that his authority would be supreme. One reason for this existed in the continuing challenges from the Ainu and other marauding bands in the northern areas of Honshu. Thus Yoritomo selected the little rustic fishing village of Kamakura, at the edge of the Kanto plain (about thirty-five miles from present-day Tokyo) as his *Bakufu,* or "army headquarters." The term *Bakufu* came in time to stand for the military government at Kamakura in general, as well as for the headquarters of the military ruler and the location of his power. In 1192 Yoritomo had the emperor name him *Seii-tai-shōgun,* "barbarian-suppressing-generalissimo," which shortly became simply *shōgun,* or "generalissimo." From that moment until 1868 the shōgun or shōgunate became the standard name for the hereditary military dictatorship in Japan.

Yoritomo established a new system of rule for his newly won territories. He made standard the practice that based the holding of land on a contract of personal loyalty. This custom had been gradually emerging in the countryside. The shōgun rewarded knights and other nobles who had joined him, when he swept over the country from his rural Kanto base, by assigning them lands of the defeated Taira or by naming them "protectors" or managers of the estates that had been loyal to him. What emerged was a genuine feudalism: that is, the system of assigning land control based upon a set of mutual obligations and centered on an oath of loyalty. In return for the personal loyalty given to him, the shōgun gave an assigned portion of the produce of the land and protection through membership in the warrior caste. Japan's new system resembled very closely the feudalism in full flower in Europe at that time. In fact, it was the only authentic feudalism to develop anywhere in Asia. And it seemed ideally suited to the boldness and ferocity of the times.

Though some of the former civil bureaucracy, based in Kyoto, persisted, because members of the imperial family continued to hold large estates or manors, Yoritomo's simple pattern of rule quickly took hold. It required a minimum amount of government apparatus, since all that was necessary was to place one of his loyal retainers in each province or

estate throughout the land. This system could lead to problems, however, because it was naturally difficult to ensure continuing loyalty as generations changed; yet because of the important role the Japanese assigned to family lines and inherited traditions and the intense feelings they developed about loyalty, the rule under Yoritomo's feudalism from Kamakura gave Japan a fairly stable and effective government for almost a century and a half.

The Kamakura period, one of the most influential in Japanese national history, lasted until 1333, when once again the center of power returned to Kyoto. It gave national approval to the emergence of the military knights, the *samurai* (literally, "one who serves"), as a special privileged class in the society. In the headquarters of the shōgun a new style developed—the simplicity and austerity of the military camp—and although some of the Buddhist sects from Kyoto were to locate their temples near the Bakufu in an attempt to gain influence over the shōgun and his lieutenants, it was the values of the armed and courageous warrior rather than the court aristocrat that came to dominate a new mode in Japanese art and literature. The Buddhists did succeed, however, in gaining support for the erection of another immense bronze statue of Amida in the middle of the thirteenth century. This Great Buddha at Kamakura, though not so high in artistic quality as the one cast in Nara five hundred years before, is an impressive sight and is visited every day by Japanese and foreign tourists. Its sheer bulk, the fact that it is unsheltered, and the less refined lines of the casting help to make it a fitting symbol of the Kamakura period.

The samurai as a class have been compared to the knights of Europe, but there were many differences between the two. In Japan, for example, there were no notions about a special chivalry toward women. The

The great Buddha at Kamakura, made of copper and gold and one of the most outstanding Buddhist sculptures in Japan

Japanese were clad in light and flexible armor, equally strong but not as clumsy as that of their European counterparts. Their armor was made of thin steel strips held together by silken cords. But it was their swords that gave them the greatest status. Japanese swords of the thirteenth century were made from the finest steel in the whole world. They were crafted by men who, through generations of family tradition, had learned to combine metal alloys in such a way as to ensure razor-sharp and incomparably strong edges and at the same time the flexibility of softer steels. Only the samurai could carry swords, which were thought to be endowed with almost mystical powers. The samurai family placed a sword at the bedside of the new infant heir and the sword was symbolically present at the deathbed of an aged warrior. Japanese warriors brandished their swords with a ferocity and disciplined ability that made their battles awesome affairs.

Before the samurai, who struck terror in the hearts of the poor peasants, commoners had no rights. The Japanese knights could demand and expect services and attention. For their own part, however, they spent long hours in training, ritual, meditation, and a spartan life in the countryside. Around the *bushi,* or warriors, grew a whole style of ritual conduct, which later became known as *Bushidō,* or "the way of the warrior." Maximum value was placed upon stoic bravery. The warrior who feared death or injury was no warrior at all. Above all, death was preferable to disgrace, any indication of cowardice, or failure to give absolute loyalty. Suicide was also preferable to capture and the threatened beheading which that would bring. The brave act of *harakiri,* or the Japanese form of suicide by slitting open one's own abdomen, came to be regarded as an honorable way of escape from any situation that could be regarded as a disgraceful one.

In feudal Japan, loyalty to one's lord was personal and deeply felt; it became the overriding virtue. When the samurai fought with each other, each contestant would proclaim his proud ancestry, the wonders of his sword and its history of victories, and the name of the lord for whom he fought in the right cause. Samurai tended to respect each other and regard fellow members of the class as brothers. Sometimes their loyalty to each other, and always their personal commitment to their lord, would take precedence over concern for family or any earthly possessions. The samurai was expected to sacrifice home, family, and everything without hesitation when called upon.

Not surprisingly, during the Kamakura period there developed a whole new body of literature stressing the austere and disciplined lives of military heroes. Such works as the *Tale of the Heike,* a romance full of episodes of bravery and heroism, as well as pathos, that occurred during the course of the three final decades of struggle between the Taira and the Minamoto, added to the romanticism of the cult of the samurai. Like its predecessor *The Tale of Genji,* which dealt primarily with court life, this new romance dealing with the epic battles became the inspiration for scroll paintings. These paintings show vivid scenes of combat, the burning of palaces, and the individual samurai in their battle attire looking especially fearsome. Many of the tales of this vigorous age were told in ballad form and often were chanted with musical accompaniment. They reinforced a romantic view that the ethical code of the samurai class was a model for all society, a view that was to last well into the nineteenth century and in some respects up to the present day. Japanese loyalty to their employers in modern industrial society stems from values that were inculcated in the Kamakura period.

Reinforcement for the national spirit of the warrior caste came from new and more broadly based and popular Buddhist teachings that spread from China during Kamakura times. The Buddhist leaders who began to preach that elaborate ceremonies and ritual were not necessary for salvation and that it was only necessary to call out the name of the

*Over: dressing in
samurai armor*

Amida Buddha for salvation and entrance into the "Western Paradise" found a favorable audience. The monk Honen founded the Jōdo, or "Pure Land," sect in 1175, urging his followers to recite incessantly the name of Amida. His student Shinran taught that just one sincere invocation of Amida could bring salvation and this could extend to prayers for others. These two men did much to popularize Buddhism among the masses. Many warriors were happy to recite the name of Amida as they went into battle, having been reassured this would save them from the terrors of hell, which were pictured in very grim detail in those days. To this day the Jōdo sect remains one of the most powerful in Japan.

A Buddhist leader who became a national figure during the Kamakura period was Nichiren (1222–1282). He founded a movement based on an old Indian text, the Lotus Sutra, and used a revivalist style of preaching to denounce moral degeneration among the people and the other sects. He was one of the first Japanese to speak and write about the fate of the "nation," and he insisted that the national future was linked to purifying all the people through his Hokke ("Lotus") sect. Nichiren predicted that unless the nation got rid of corrupting influences, by which he meant his rivals, it would be punished by foreign invasion. His was one of the very few intolerant approaches to religious faith in Japanese history. For his denunciations he incurred the displeasure of the Bakufu government and was sent into exile, only to return even more fired by fanatical fervor.

But the sect with the most impact on Japan in Kamakura times was Zen. It has left an indelible stamp on Japanese society and culture. *Zen* comes from an Indian word that means "meditation." Zen, like most Japanese sects, came from China, but it seemed tailor-made for the society that had just emerged. The Japanese embraced it and adapted

Modern Japanese dressed as samurai for a festival

it so intensely that it became a pervading part of the whole culture, part of the national spirit, even though it appealed mainly to the samurai at first.

Zen taught that "enlightenment," the essence of the approach to ultimate truth or *nirvana,* lay within the self. Enlightenment came like a sudden burst of light and could help the spirit jump over an endless series of struggles toward an almost instantaneous salvation. Enlightenment was not to be found in expensive ritual or the scriptures of philosophical speculation, said the masters of Zen, but by intense concentration and self-examination, in a simple and nondistracting atmosphere. The moment of enlightenment would come only after a long period of rigorous training and apprenticeship, including emphasis on physical control and intense concentration. Zen masters demanded strict obedience of their disciples and inflicted corporal punishment on them for the slightest infraction.

It is not difficult to understand why Zen seemed especially designed for the samurai. While the common people were reciting the name of Amida, the warrior class adopted Zen almost as their own special religion in Kamakura times. Zen taught the unimportance of the Buddhist texts, which appealed to a group who tended to be generally rustic and illiterate. Ideas of discipline and austerity fitted in admirably with the military spirit. Physical control and concentration were the hallmarks of a good swordsman. Zen training also emphasized that essential characteristic of the military life, obedience.

It was a good thing the Japanese were able to develop their military spirit during the first century of the Kamakura era, because their abilities were to be sorely tested by the attempted invasion of which Nichiren had warned. Throughout Europe and Asia in the thirteenth century, terror was struck by the great Mongol conquests. The descendants of Genghis Khan ranged from the gates of Vienna and Baghdad to Vietnam, and they conquered all of China. Kublai Khan, who ascended the throne in China, sent a message to the Japanese demand-

tached to Yoritomo could no longer be claimed by those who ruled in the name of the Bakufu. Japan tended to split into independent small military principalities sustained by their samurai.

The Kamakura pattern of rule ended in 1333. Then, for the last time, a prince of the royal family attempted to restore its power to govern. But such was not to be the political pattern in Japan. Within five years a member of the Ashikaga family had himself named shōgun. He and his successors spent most of the remaining years of the fourteenth century attempting to exercise control over the country. Though they managed to remain shōguns until the end of the fifteenth century, when the country lapsed into civil war, their power never approached that of the Bakufu at Kamakura. None of the samurai, except those personally pledged to the Ashikaga, owed loyalty. This was a sad period in Japanese history in some respects, one of almost constant warfare, in which the chief victims were the Japanese peasants.

But there was also a bright side, for the aftermath of the Mongol invasions had ushered in a period of great change. The Japanese began to be interested in seafaring and trading, and numerous small port cities grew up to engage in active trade with China and Korea. From some of the towns, encouraged by the local barons, the Japanese ventured forth as pirates to prey upon the great treasure-laden Chinese junks or to send raiding parties ashore to pilfer Chinese seacoast towns. The booty quickly found its way to the homes of the feudal leaders.

Though in the early days of their shōgunate the Ashikaga rulers had fought numerous campaigns to bring the country once again under a centralized control, by the early 1400s they had settled into an acceptance of the relative independence of the great *daimyō*. The *daimyō* in turn began to pay less attention to fighting for a while and joined in the pleasantnesses of life in the capital and in their growing fortress towns.

The Ashikaga fell prey to what Yoritomo had feared two centuries before and had avoided: they were enticed by the beauties of court life in Kyoto. They built themselves sumptuous palaces with handsome gardens in the northwestern part of the city, known as the Muromachi sector. The period from 1392 to 1573 in Japanese history under the Ashikaga is usually known as the Muromachi period because of the new and luxurious style it ushered in. The shōgun's family was joined in Kyoto by many of the *daimyō,* who decided to build town houses and participate in the excitement of life there.

These were sad days for the imperial and other royal families. Many of their lands were confiscated by the powerful feudal lords, and the new rich men in the capital were too interested in enjoying themselves to consider support for the court nobility. For more than thirty years in the first half of the sixteenth century there was no properly installed emperor, because the court was too poor to carry out necessary coronation ceremonies. But no one seemed to notice. One emperor, highly educated in the classical tradition, was forced to sell pieces of his beautiful calligraphy to the rich feudal barons and their followers in order to feed himself.

This was also a time of renewed cultural brilliance for China, which had expelled its foreign overlords, the Mongols, and established a new Chinese dynasty, the Ming, in 1368. As always, the Japanese were interested in developments in China, and the shōgunate, as well as the feudal lords, sought Chinese products through both trade and piracy. But this time the Japanese tended to approach the Chinese as equals; after all, they had defeated the Mongols and the Chinese had not.

The Muromachi period became the age when Japanese culture, with all the conflicting background influences, came into full flower. It represented a compromise between the more vigorous style of the feudal warriors, with their enthusiasm for Zen, and the court style of the past, with its delicacy, sensitivity, and love for things Chinese. It was made possible by the remarkable flourishing of trade and craft guilds and the enthusiasm that the feudal barons brought to their discovery of the importance of cultural values. This was one of the most creative periods in Japanese history—a truly Japanese period. It was at the height of the flourishing under the Ashikaga that the Jesuits first encountered Japan. Little wonder they were struck by the elegance and the high stage of development.

Interestingly enough, the principal underlying inspiration for the cultural development during the Muromachi came from Zen. The Zen monks had also changed and had become some of the leading activists and scholars of the time. Though emphasis on discipline continued to characterize their approach, the Zen monks branched into all sorts of activities. Their schools became some of the best centers for the study of Chinese culture, and the Zen monasteries were remarkable for the simple lines and the natural beauty of their architecture. Zen monks also helped in the financing of trading expeditions. On every side of Ashikaga life the influence of Zen could be felt.

Nowhere was this more important than in the development of Japanese gardens. The Zen teachers emphasized simplicity and that natural beauty should be contemplated in order to become enlightened about the world. Their disciples sculptured rock gardens, sand gardens, and little areas where the world could be seen in miniature. Under Zen inspiration, Japanese gardeners became the world's finest. In Muromachi times it became essential to plan the building and the surrounding gardens at the same time so that they could blend perfectly with each other in a natural setting. Many of the most beautiful gardens and associated structures in the world can be seen in Kyoto today. They date from Muromachi times and are still meticulously cared for. One is the famous Golden Pavilion, which was built by the Shōgun Yoshimitsu for his retirement in 1394. It fits into a beautiful natural surrounding in such a way that the visitor feels as if it has always been there.

Zen monks also initiated the Japanese tea ceremony, and during Ashikaga times this disciplined ceremonial pattern for the meeting of friends to admire a view or a work of art became highly stylized. Like

Zen itself, it required intense concentration, physical control, and aesthetic abilities. Many small pavilions were built in Japanese gardens especially for the performance of this elaborate ritual.

Muromachi also witnessed the development of the Nō drama, a distinctly Japanese form of entertainment with simple stage and classic stories acted out in slow precision to the beat of a drum and the plaintive sound of a bamboo flute. Nō acting, like Zen training, takes years of practice, and Japanese today respect highly those older Nō performers who carry on the tradition. The costumes, as befitted the Muromachi period, are elaborate and colorful. The masks worn by the actors are frequently considered to be artistic masterpieces of great value.

Throughout Japan, the Muromachi style of Kyoto spread rapidly. Art and architecture in the outlying provinces mimicked the gardens and temples of Kyoto and the famous landscape paintings of the Kyoto artists. Today much of the Muromachi style, with its beautiful porcelains, paintings, buildings, and gardens, is preserved intact in Kyoto. Art lovers from all over the world travel there to see Japanese culture at its own high peak of achievement.

Artistic creativity and the sophisticated life of Kyoto did not, however, stop the intermittent battles for power among the *daimyō*. The cult of the warrior caste continued along with disruption until the great feudal lord Tokugawa Ieyasu unified the country under a very strict and more centralized form of feudalism and proclaimed a new shōgunate in 1603. Beginning then, Japan passed out of its ancient period and was in the throes of change toward a new national unity.

*Realistic portrait in lacquered wood
of a Zen priest, abbot of a monastery
in the Muromachi period*

UNDERSTANDING TRADITIONAL JAPAN
ITS LIFE AND ITS IMPORTANCE

We have now seen how the Japanese, isolated in general from the mainstream of developments in Asia, were able to develop over the centuries a unique culture and pattern of life. Their organized energy, their discipline, their restraint, and, above all, their native artistic capacities enabled them to develop their society with remarkable unity and attention to aesthetic standards. By the twelfth century many of the Japanese customs had become deeply ingrained. Their approach to nature, to their fellow men, and to their interpretation of the divine plan that seemed to organize their daily routine seemed settled. Japan, a truly unusual pattern in human development, was already in a position to offer much to the rest of the world.

In this traditional Japanese society, it is important to understand that inequality was accepted, and people were expected to accept the calling or station into which they were born. The Japanese attention to *uji,* or clan origins, had been reinforced by the Buddhist doctrine of fate. There was a great gap between the ruling classes and the commoners, with little chance for change of status. In addition to the royal family and some of the other noble families frequently claiming ancestral relationship to it, the samurai counted as a special privileged group. The great feudal barons, usually of samurai origin, and their samurai defenders constituted a class apart in society. They were entitled to rights that those below them did not dare to hope for. Not only did they have the exclusive right to wear the swords symbolizing their authority, but they also had servants and a food allowance and were entitled to expect quarters at any inn along the highway. Purity of samurai blood was initially kept by ensuring that marriages were between members of the same class. Samurai behavior, including the disciplined bearing, tended to reinforce respect for authority and class origins in the feudal society. When members of this class passed along the paths linking the Japanese towns, the lower classes sank to their knees and touched their faces to the ground. The present-day custom of bowing low comes from such early habits of strict attention to rank in society. Class consciousness persists in Japan, and family origins dating back to ancient times dictate how Japanese behave toward each other.

Below the nobility and warrior class came the peasants, artisans, and merchants, in that order. Ancient Japan also had slaves and "outcasts" (*eta*). The latter sometimes included the "hairy Ainu"; these people were assigned the unclean tasks, such as being butchers or leather manufacturers, which the traditional emphasis on purity made undesirable for the members of the Yamato race. Though there was some movement back and forth between classes during the Ashikaga period —a few of the peasants who joined in fighting the Mongol invaders, for example, managed to work their way into the samurai class—distinctions remained fairly rigid. It would be difficult to understand Japanese behavior in the twentieth century without appreciating that the Japanese still place great emphasis on family and class origins.

Though in early Japan the family inheritance was divided equally among all the children, during the turbulence of the Ashikaga period it became customary for the head of the family to designate one heir so that the family holdings could be kept together and protected. The father did not necessarily choose the eldest son, but the one with most promise, and the rest of the family was expected to support the choice. Sometimes, if no promising son could be found, the father might adopt a talented male relative or son of a friend as his heir, and again, the family was expected to support the selection. Thus, especially in the fourteenth and fifteenth centuries, the Japanese developed an emphasis on the family as a basic social and economic unit with individual members bound in loyalty and service to the family's male head. This marked a beginning of the subordinate position for women that can still be observed in modern Japan. Members of the household were expected to obey orders from the head of the family, whether he was their father, their brother, or an adopted outsider.

The backbone of the whole Japanese system was the peasantry, who constituted more than three quarters of the population. The peasants' life was generally hard and bitter. They were frequently subjected to unfair taxes; their crops were all too often either destroyed or confiscated by warring bands (the major crop, rice, is one of the most labor-demanding of all agricultural products); and sometimes they were subject to the floods and ravages of typhoons. The peasants raised mulberry trees for silkworms, tea, vegetables, fruits, hemp, and, of course, grains. Though their lot was harsh, the peasants were given a higher social status than elsewhere in Asia because so much depended upon their success in providing food for the upper classes. The Japanese seasons and therefore the crops were generally reliable; Japan seldom has excessive dry spells during the growing season. The Japanese peasants were also usually close enough to the Pacific Ocean or nearby inland seas to be able to supplement their diet with fish. Fish has always been the major protein in Japanese food. Then, too, Japanese peasants always had an abundant supply of bamboo to help them with their building and other activities. The designs for bamboo umbrellas, fans, ladles, and ornaments by Japanese peasants have combined usefulness and natural form and have continued to provide some standard items for everyday life. Nor must we forget that Japanese farmers could always feast their eyes on the remarkable natural beauties of the country.

With the development of towns, either in connection with the growing trade with Korea and China or around the headquarters of the great feudal leaders, craftsmen and merchants assumed greater impor-

*Working in the rice paddies much as it was
done hundreds of years ago in front of a farmhouse
that has not changed over the centuries*

tance. Later, as they accumulated wealth, they were to look down upon the simple peasants as ignorant and uncultured. The various craftsmen organized themselves into guilds or *za* with their own secrets, systems of apprenticeship, and specialized language. These included, for example, carpenters, roofers, plasterers, tatami-makers, and dyers. The blacksmiths and swordsmiths were especially important, as their products had an almost sacred quality. Sons were expected to follow in the trade of their fathers.

Because it was felt they contributed little to society, merchants were traditionally placed below the craftsmen on the social scale. After all, a sword sharpener performed a vital service for the samurai, whereas the merchant who sold silk cloth, it was sometimes felt, tried to take advantage of the warrior. By the end of the Ashikaga period, however, a number of great Japanese merchant families had developed and had proved sufficiently astute to be able to buy into the samurai class by convenient marriages arranged for their daughters or by lending money to the great *daimyō,* whose expensive tastes frequently caused them financial difficulties.

Although some of the *daimyō* and noble families built beautiful homes and gardens during the Muromachi period, life in Japan remained essentially austere and simple. Yet the Japanese, of all peoples in the world, managed best to blend the simplicity of their homes and gardens into the beauties of nature's surroundings. Today many of the leading architectural and landscape gardening firms in the West employ Japanese specialists to help them. The skills and the aesthetic approach these citizens of Japan bring to their work trace back to early times in their country. Many of the features giving qualities of lightness and airiness to modern homes in the West are directly traceable to Japanese influence.

The Japanese have themselves retained many of the basic features that characterized the living style of early times, and especially the disciplined simplicity of the Ashikaga period. In an age of modern skyscrapers and concrete and steel buildings, they still insist on the soft qualities of natural wood and the lightness of paper for interior decoration. A visitor can enter a restaurant within a modern structure in Tokyo today and find that the Japanese have arranged it in a manner that is little different from what it would have been many centuries ago.

Except for electricity and some modern conveniences, the Japanese have also clung to the ancient traditions for their homes or modern apartments. Japan is a small country, and the houses and living areas in the towns tended to be small too. The essential features of the Japanese homes were—and are still—neatness, convenience, cleanliness, and restraint. There was always a small area where dirty outer footgear could be removed before moving up a step into the living area. Japanese still remove their shoes in a vestibule before entering a home. Mattresses were unrolled on the soft tatami (in peasant homes they were simply straw mats on the ground) floors at night and were neatly put away in the cupboards during the day so that the family could sit in comfort, usually cross-legged for the men and a kneeling position for the women. Thus the same room served as living room and bedroom. The area had a lightness and airiness provided by a soft wooden framework with sliding paper-covered panels that could easily be removed to let in the sunlight. These panels, called *shoji,* are a standard feature in all Japanese decor today, lending a warmth and atmosphere of intimacy to the surroundings.

In some of the samurai homes, and later in those of the rich merchants, it became a standard practice to set aside a little alcove, perhaps only three feet square (about half the size of a tatami mat), where in a most simple manner a family treasure, such as a vase, a painting, a wood carving, or a fine piece of lacquer, could be shown. This small area, or *tokonoma,* became a standard feature of the Japanese home. It was inspired in part by the austere discipline associated with early Zen Buddhism. The idea was to purify one's thoughts by the uncluttered

concentration on a single work of beauty. To the Japanese mind, to put a variety of pieces into this nook would detract from the appreciation of a single art treasure and probably from the aesthetic beauty of the home itself. Families wealthy enough to have several art treasures would change the work displayed in the *tokonoma* from time to time.

Equally important in the ancient and modern Japanese home, no matter how humble, is some sort of small garden—a little world in miniature. Through their gardens the people express their closeness to nature, their sense of proportion, and their ability to blend their lives with the seasons.

Japanese meals match the single-story simplicity of the homes. They were, and are, usually served on small lacquer trays about eighteen inches square and about nine inches high. Though the diet is humble, consisting usually of colorful pickled vegetables, a piece of fish, dried seaweed, a thin soup, and rice, great attention is given to artistic arrangement, as befits the natural inclination of the people. The Japanese learned from the Chinese the use of chopsticks (*hashi* in Japanese), but with the exception of the rice, the style and taste of the meals are distinctly their own. One common item in most Japanese meals is *miso*, a fermented soybean paste, a frequent basic flavoring as well as nourishment in the soups. From very earliest times *miso* lent a distinctive flavor to the native cuisine.

If life was rugged for all except the privileged few at the top of the social pyramid, there were nevertheless forms of entertainment to provide some happy occasions for the peasants and townsfolk. One popular attraction was *sumō*, a form of wrestling and an ancient sport originally performed at temples and shrines. But most important were the various festivals such as the celebration of the lunar New Year or the midsummer Buddhist *bon* dances and processions. The *bon* dances and songs and sumō have survived to the present as a part of the culture.

Classic Japanese costume,
still worn today, for a Nō play

*Making rice cakes
in the old way*

At all festive occasions—and these could include the completion of large-scale labor projects on which all inhabitants of an area might cooperate—the Japanese enjoyed their national drink, *sake*. Sake is made of fermented rice, and the sweet-tasting drink is served warm, which tends to make it more intoxicating. The pressures of hard work within the rigid class system encouraged the Japanese in moments of gaiety and abandon. Early Chinese travelers to Japan commented that the people often partook of strong drink. But such occasions were not too frequent; the Japanese people remained remarkably conscientious and hardworking most of their waking hours.

For the people in the Land of the Rising Sun customs became formalized and stylized, and it has usually been difficult for the outside observer to penetrate beneath surface appearances. These surface appearances were every bit as important as the substance, though, and for the Japanese, outward signs represented the inner control of the spirit by the self. The behavior of the Japanese is still the most immediate and telling indication of the degree to which the cultural traditions from a distant past have penetrated into every aspect of their lives. The outward signs that visitors have come to admire in the Japanese as a people include emphasis on ceremony and manners, cleanliness, balance and simplicity, conscientious hard work, and an artistic ability to capture the meaning of nature. These are signs of those inner qualities of character such as integrity and loyalty that reflect the good life.

Twentieth-century Japan has been acclaimed as a modern miracle, and in many respects it is. On the surface other people would not expect that so much from early times had been retained, but it has. The Japanese still have a system of indirect rule. The emperor reigns but does not have real power. The people are still sensitive toward and attentive to what goes on in China, but they maintain their insular detachment. Within the society, the discipline of the labor force and its loyalty to the modern industrial corporation bespeak values inculcated by samurai traditions. The Japanese appreciation of the importance of

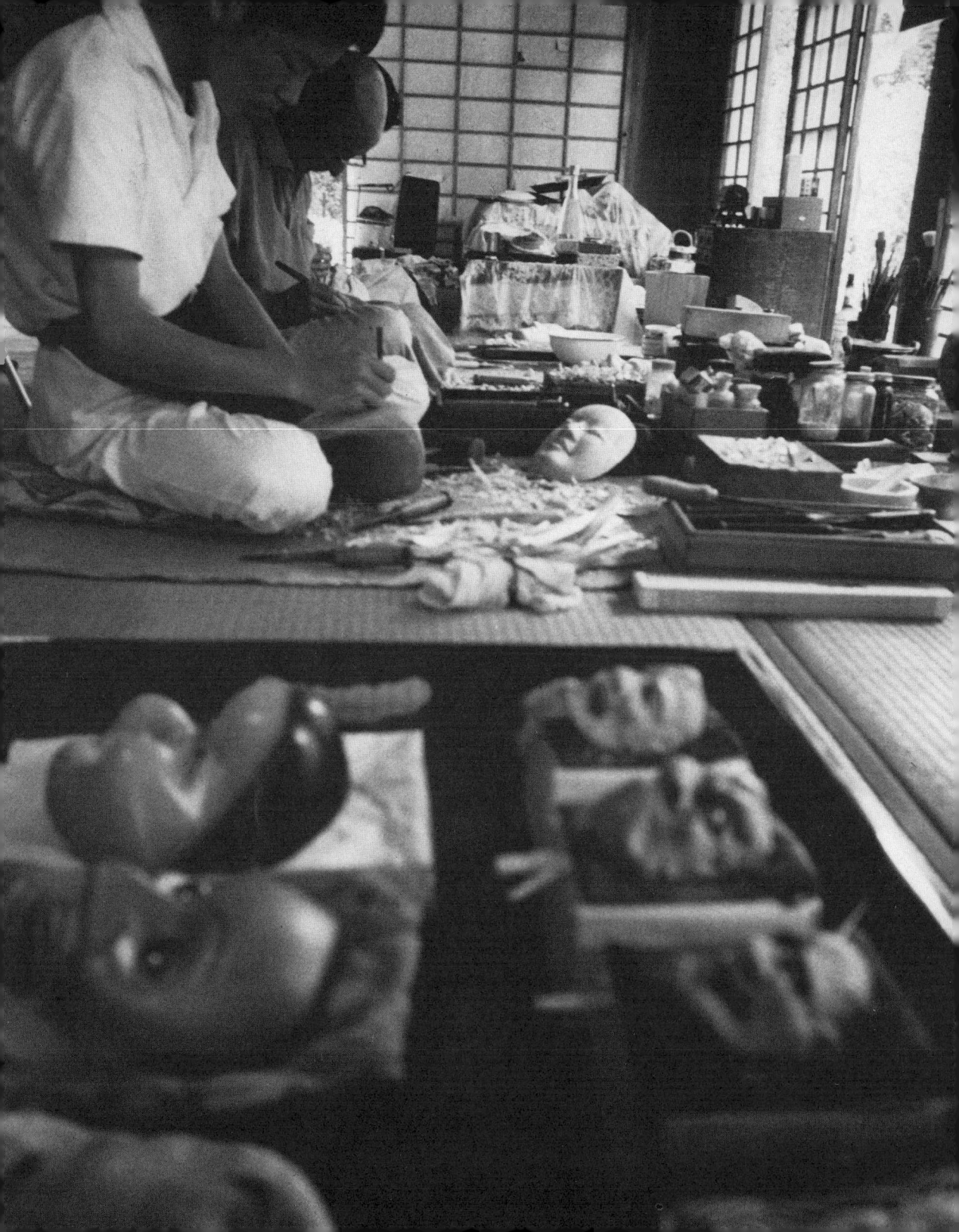

trade for their national economy today dates from the Ashikaga times and the growth of a seafaring tradition. But most of all, the qualities of Japanese life and aesthetic values stem from their own insular and usually isolated cultural traditions. These traditions have also included attention to legends and shrines, as any visitor can quickly discover today. These are in turn related to the continuing love for pomp and ceremony and pageantry. At almost any season there is opportunity to observe a religious or folk festival in Japan. Most of these can be traced back to the earliest times. They are a way of ensuring that the traditions from the ancient past remain alive.

Once Japan came into full contact with the modern industrialized West in the nineteenth century, it was ready again for the process of adopt, adapt, adept. But meanwhile its people had been willed a legacy that enabled them to contribute an enrichment to the rest of the world —in art, literature, gardens, and especially in putting man into proper relationship with nature.

Workers sitting on tatami are painting masks for Nō plays

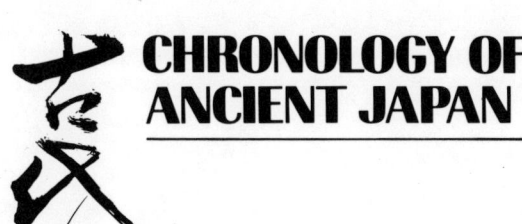

CHRONOLOGY OF ANCIENT JAPAN

B.C. 4000–250		*Jomon Period*
	660	Legendary date of founding of Japan by Jimmu
B.C. 250– A.D. 250		*Yayoi Period*
		Introduction of rice, iron, bronze, and arts from China
A.D.	5	Enshrining of sacred mirror at Ise
c. 250–538		*Tomb Culture Period*
		Migration of horsemen from northeast Asia
538–710		*Classical Period and Chinese Borrowing*
	604	"Constitution" of Prince Shōtoku
	607	First official expedition to China (last in 836)
	645–650	The Taika or "Great Reforms" of Nakatomi
710–794		*Nara Period*
	710	Building of first great capital for Japan
	712–720	Writing of national histories *Kojiki* and *Nihongi*
794–857		*Heian Period*
	794	Capital founded at Heian (modern Kyoto)
		Chinese-style art and poetry
857–1185		*Fujiwara Period*
		Development of *Kana* makes possible national literature
	1020	Lady Murasaki writes *Tale of Genji,* world's first novel
	1160	Taira family wins over Minamoto in prolonged war
1185–1338		*Kamakura Period*
		Yoritomo establishes military headquarters at Kamakura and a feudal system

1192	Yoritomo named shōgun
1274, 1281	Kublai Khan's two attempted invasions defeated
1338–1597	*Ashikaga Shōgunate*
	Ashikaga move headquarters back to Kyoto
1392–1573	Muromachi period, high achievement of Japanese national style in art, literature, and life
1542	Portuguese and Jesuits arrive
1600	Ieyasu Tokugawa wins Battle of Sekigahara and founds (1603) TOKUGAWA SHŌGUNATE

BIBLIOGRAPHY

Cressey, George B. *Asia's Lands and Peoples.* 3rd ed. New York: McGraw-Hill, 1963.

Dunn, Charles J. *Everyday Life in Traditional Japan.* Rutland, Vt.: Charles E. Tuttle, 1969.

Hall, John W. *Government and Local Power in Japan, 500 to 1700.* Princeton, N.J.: Princeton University Press, 1966.

Keene, Donald. *Japanese Literature: An Introduction for Western Readers.* New York: Grove Press, 1955.

Leonard, Jonathan N. *Early Japan.* New York: Time-Life Books, 1968.

Murasaki, Lady. *The Tale of Genji,* Translated by Arthur Waley. New York: Modern Library, 1960.

Paine, Robert T., and Soper, Alexander. *The Art and Architecture of Japan.* Rev. ed. Baltimore: Penguin Books, 1960.

Reischauer, Edwin O. *Japan, Past and Present.* 3rd rev. ed. New York: Alfred A. Knopf, 1964.

Reischauer, Edwin O., and Fairbank, John K. *East Asia: The Great Tradition.* Boston: Houghton Mifflin, 1960.

Sansom, George B. *Japan: A Short Cultural History.* New York: Appleton-Century-Crofts, 1962.

Suzuki, D. T. *Zen and Japanese Culture.* New York: Pantheon Books, 1959.

Tsunoda, Ryusaku; de Bary, William Theodore; and Keene, Donald. *Sources of the Japanese Tradition.* New York: Columbia University Press, 1958.

Waley, Arthur. *Nō Plays of Japan.* New York: Alfred A. Knopf, 1922.

Walker, Richard L. *Ancient China.* New York: Franklin Watts, Inc., 1969.

INDEX

Agriculture and gardens, 7, 10, 16, 28, 41, 63, 68, 70
Ainu people, 5, 46, 47, 67
Amaterasu. *See* Gods, goddesses
Amida (Amida Buddha), 27, 49, 55, 56
Ancient records. *See* Historians, histories
Animists, 11, 13
Architecture, 8, 28, 36, 41, 70
Art, arts, 8, 10, 28, 31, 33, 35, 36, 37, 38, 41, 49, 51, 62, 63, 65, 73
Artifacts, 16
Ashikaga, family and period, 61, 62, 63, 67, 70, 77

Bakufu ("army headquarters," military government), 47, 49, 55, 60, 61
Bamboo, 8, 10, 68
Bodhisattvas, 24, 27
Buddhism, 20–45, 49, 51, 55, 56, 66, 73
Bushidō, 50

Calendar system, 23
Calligraphy, 37, 38
Carbon-14 tests, 14, 16
Ch'ang-an (Sian), China, 31, 32, 33

China and influence on Japan, 2, 5, 16, 18, 19, 20–45, 55, 58, 60, 61, 68, 75
Chinese fashion, 20
Christian Era, 4, 5, 7, 14, 20, 23, 24
Civil service, 33, 47
Civilization, age of Japanese, 2
Clan origins, 66, 67
Class consciousness, 67
   See also Japan: traditional
Classical Age, 20–45
Cleanliness as tradition, 1, 13
Climate, 10
Confucius, 23, 24, 31
Costumes, 2, 11, 36, 65
Craftsmen, 14, 16
Culture, development of, 4
Customs, 1, 2, 4, 7, 8, 14, 66, 70

Daimyō (military lords), 61, 62, 65, 70
Destiny, feeling of, 2
Discipline, 1
Dynasties, 19

Eastern Seas Circuit, 32
Eclecticism, 21

Festivals, 11, 75, 77

Feudalism, 47, 50, 51–61, 62, 65, 66
Food, 2, 68, 73, 75
Fuji, Mt., 10
Fujiwara, family and period, 32, 42, 43

Gardens. *See* Agriculture and gardens
Genghis Khan. *See* Mongol conquests
Genji, Prince (in *The Tale of Genji*), 38
Genji family, 45
Genshin, 27
Geography, 2, 5, 8, 10, 21
Gods, goddesses, 13, 14, 21, 33
Grand Shrine, Ise, 14
Great Reform (Taika), 32

Harakiri, 50
Heian (Heian-kyo; now Kyoto), 35, 42
    See also Kyoto
Heian period, 37, 42
Hikari Express, 1
Historians, histories, 33
Hokkaido, 8
Hokke sect, 55
Homes, 2, 42, 70, 73
Honen (monk), 55
Honshu, 8, 14, 43, 45, 47
Hōryū-ji temple, 24

Imperial families, 7, 13, 16, 18, 21, 32, 35, 42, 46, 47, 75
India, 31, 55
Industry, 16, 28, 68, 70, 75, 77
Ise, 13, 14
Isolation of Japan, 2, 16, 66

Japan
  to A.D. 538, 1–19
  Classical Age, 20–45
  military society, 46–65
  traditional, 66–77
Japanese Chronicle. *See* Historians, histories
Jesuits, 4, 13, 63
Jimmu Tenno, 13
Jōdo sect, 55
Jōmon period, 14, 16

Kamakura era, 47, 49, 51, 55, 56, 58, 60, 61
Kamatari, Nakatomi no, 32, 33, 42
Kamikaze, 60
Kammu, emperor, 35
Kana, syllabary, 37, 38
Kanto plain, 10, 32, 43, 46, 47
Kiyomori, 43
Kokinshū ("Collection of Ancient and Modern Poems"), 41
Korea, 5, 16, 18, 19, 20, 21, 28, 58, 60, 68
Kōya, Mt., 29
Kublai Khan. *See* Mongol conquests
Kūkai (monk), 29
Kyoto, 4, 32, 35, 36, 42, 46, 47, 49, 62, 63, 65
Kyushu, 8, 43, 46, 58, 60

Language, 5, 18, 19, 20, 21, 36, 37, 38
Literature. *See* Art, arts
Lotus Sutra movement, 55
Loyalty. *See* Feudalism

Makimono (picture scrolls), 38

[84]

Manyōshū ("Book of Ten Thousand Leaves"), 41
Merchants, 70
Middle Kingdom, 23, 29
Military society, 7, 42, 46–65
Minamoto family, 42, 43, 45
Missionaries, 4, 28
Mongol conquests, 56, 58, 60, 61, 62, 67
Mongoloids, 5, 16
Murasaki, Lady, 38, 45
Muromachi period, 62, 63, 65, 70
Myths, 11

Nara, 33, 35, 36, 37, 41
National character, 27, 28
Nature, Japanese approach to, 1, 2, 10, 11
Navigation, 28
Nichiren, 55, 60

Origins of Japanese, 4, 5
Osaka, 13

People of Japan, 4, 5, 7
Picture scrolls, 38
    See also Art, arts
Pillow Book (of Sei Shōnagon), 37, 38
Poetry, 31, 32, 36, 37, 38, 41
Politics, 42, 43

Records, ancient, 4
Religion, 7, 11, 13, 14, 16, 28, 31
    See also individual religions
Rising Sun, Land of, 8, 13, 20, 28, 75

Saga, emperor, 45
Saichō (monk), 29
Samurai, 49, 50, 51, 67, 70
    See also Military society
Scrolls. *See* Art, arts
Seventeen Article Constitution, 23
Shikoku, 8
Shingon sect, 29
Shinto religion, 11, 13, 21, 28
    See also Religion
Shōgun, 47
    See also Military society
Shōtoku, 21, 23, 24, 28, 29, 32
Sian, 31
Siberia, 5
Significance of Japan's past, 1–19
Sport, 73
Stone Age, 5
Sui dynasty, 19
Symbols, language, 37

Taika (Great Reform), 32
Taira, 42, 43, 45, 46, 47
Tale of Genji (Lady Murasaki), 38, 51
Tale of the Heike, 51
T'ang dynasty, 19, 31, 35, 36, 38
Tanka (short poems), 41
Tatami mats, 2
Taxes, 42, 43
Tenchi, emperor, 32
Tendai sect, 29
Tōdai-ji (Great Eastern Temple), 33
Tōkaidō (Eastern Seas Circuit), 32
Tokugawa Ieyasu, 65
Tokyo, 1, 16, 32, 70
Tomb culture, 16, 18

Tombs, 16, 18
Traditions, 1, 2, 7, 10, 14, 24, 27, 35
Tribes of Ancient Japan, 5, 7

Values in Japanese life, 1
Vegetation, 8, 10
Volcanos, 8

Weights and measures, 23
Western impact, 21

World power, Japan as, 2
Writing, 36–37

Yamato region, 7, 13, 29, 35, 38, 67
Yayoi period, 16, 18
Yoritomo, 43, 45, 46, 47, 49, 61
Yoshifusa, 42
Yoshimitsu, 63

Zen, 55, 56, 62, 63, 65

ABOUT THE AUTHOR

Richard L. Walker is Director of the Institute of International Studies at the University of South Carolina and a specialist on East Asia. During and after World War II, he served in the Pacific and Japan, and he has returned to that area of the world to live and travel more than twenty times since. The research for *Ancient Japan* was done while Dr. Walker was living in Kyoto, the ancient capital of Japan, and with his wife he visited many times the temples and shrines described in this book.

Dr. Walker was educated at Drew University and holds M.A. and Ph.D. degrees from Yale University. He is the author of a number of books on the Far East and has written *Ancient China: And Its Influence in the Modern World,* a companion to *Ancient Japan: And Its Influence in the Modern World.*